File Handling and other programs

for the Psion Organiser II

Other books by Mike Shaw
published by Kuma Computers Ltd:

Behind the Screens of the MSX
Using and Programming Psion Organiser II

FILE HANDLING AND OTHER PROGRAMS FOR THE PSION ORGANISER II

Mike Shaw

To Kevin, Simon, Adam, Zoe and Melanie,
and to Karen, Andrea, Vincent and Andy.

Published by
KUMA COMPUTERS LTD.

First Published 1988
Kuma Computers Ltd.
Unit 12, Horseshoe Park,
Horseshoe Road, Pangbourne,
Berkshire RG8 7JW
Telex 846741 KUMA G Tel 07357 4335

Printed in Great Britain

ISBN 07457-0135-3

Forward

Many people have purchased a Psion Organiser II for the valuable facilities it offers (the diary, address book, smart calculator and so on), to discover subsequently that they have a very powerful computer system in their hands ... a computer system capable of doing far more for them if they could only tap into its resources by using the built-in programming language.

Those with previous programming experience should find very little difficulty in getting to grips with the Organiser's language - OPL. But for the inexperienced, computer programming can seem incomprehensible: it uses a strange, almost alien language, and demands a strict adherence to precise rules. Their problem is aggravated by the fact that, for the most part, they must learn 'from the book' - with little if any outside guidance.

So how does the newcomer learn? By practice (obviously). And, strangely, by entering programs other people have written. Copying programs gives an insight into how a computer language can be used to achieve desired results. Studying how a program works enables similar programs to be written - sometimes by doing little more than making a few fairly simple changes. Examining the techniques used in a program can reveal 'tricks' for shorter and/or faster running routines.

This book is designed to help: it is not so much a tutorial on how to program, but rather a collection of routines and programs that you are invited to enter as written, and to adapt to suit your own purposes. Each routine is explained in detail, so that it may be understood and changed as required. It can be regarded as an extension of my earlier book '*Using and Programming the Psion Organiser II*' – but is in no way dependent on that book having been read.

This book concentrates on 'file-handling' routines, since file handling is probably one of the most difficult areas for the newcomer to understand – and yet it is the one most often required.

An explanation of the principles involved in handling files on the Psion Organiser is given first, followed by a variety of 'utility' routines that can be used in file-handling (and other) programs. This is followed by a demonstration of their use with two fairly comprehensive examples of file handling programs. These cover maintaining a Stock Control/Price List, and a Bank Account Handler. Both programs can be adapted to suit a variety of other applications: for example the Stock Control/Price List program can easily be adapted to handle a Stamp Collection or a Club Membership list.

The Bank Account Handler demonstrates the use of having two files in operation at a time – and shows how a file can be 'updated' automatically by using Organiser's internal calendar. The short routines used in these programs have been specially designed so that they can be adapted and incorporated in your own file handling programs without too much effort – thus making such programs easier to prepare.

There is also a number of other 'stand-alone' programs which you may find useful.

It should perhaps be mentioned that there is never just one way to achieve a result. Ask 100 people to write a program to perform a specific task, and you will get 100 different answers. Some solutions will be short. Some will be fast in operation. Some will be very 'user-friendly' – that is, give clear and meaningful messages.

Furthermore, with very few exceptions practically every program can be improved to suit a particular individual's requirements. There is a saying among programmers that a program is never finished: it is only in an advanced state of completion. No claim is made that the routines and programs in this book are the fastest or the shortest possible: they have been written to combine, as far as possible, understandability with space saving, and to demonstrate some fairly common programming techniques.

All the routines and programs in this book were written, developed and 'de-bugged' on a PC using Psion's Organiser Developer, then downloaded into a 16k Organiser Model XP (Version 2.4) and a 32k Model XP (Version 3.3), and verified before being loaded, unchanged, into the Word Processor. The printing has been taken directly from the Word Processor files using Desk Top Publishing. Thus, every effort has been made to ensure that there have been no changes and hence no errors in the listings. Furthermore, to avoid any potential mishaps through user mis-entry, 'machine-coding' techniques have not been used at all, even though in some instances these could have resulted in shorter and faster running programs. You are at liberty to adapt the programs listed in this book to suit your own purposes – indeed, you are encouraged to do so – the only proviso being that they are for your own use only, and are not sold or passed on to others.

Happy programming!

Mike Shaw
September 1988

CONTENTS

CHAPTER 2 File Handling Functions

5.8 When's Easter?

APPENDIX 1 OPL Commands and Functions

APPENDIX 2 Index of Routines

CHAPTER 1

File Handling Theory

1.1 The Principles

What is a computer file?

Depending on who you are and how you work, you will have your own concepts of what a file comprises: to a solicitor, it could be all of the correspondence and information related to an individual case; to an estate agent it could be the information related to a particular property; to an accountant it could be the facts and figures related to a particular client.

Files of a similar nature or category will be grouped – perhaps in one drawer or section of a filing cabinet. The estate agent, for example, may keep together all the properties that are within a specific price band. The objective, of course, is to make searching through the files for a particular item easier.

A computer file used to store facts and figures can be likened in many respects to a card index system, where all the information related to one record is kept on one card. There is, however, a fundamental difference between a computer file and a card-index system – a difference that gives computer maintained files a clear advantage. (This is particularly true where the Organiser is concerned). With a card-index system, the order of the cards within the box is determined by the prime search requirement. To give a simple example, index cards used to keep names and addresses are most likely to be maintained in alphabetical order, based on the name: it's not much fun having to search through every single card to find Joe Blogg's address. With a computer such as the Organiser, however, the order of the cards is almost irrelevant, since the time it takes to search through every record is insignificant.

This difference is particularly important when other criteria determine the search requirement. Taking the example of the alphabetically stored name and address cards again, to search for people living in a specific town takes the computer no longer than searching for people with the same name. You will no doubt have experienced already the speed with which your Organiser can locate information using the FIND command on the built-in filing system. To all intents and purposes, the information you require is located instantly.

Computer files have 'fields'

Let us take the card index box analogy a little further. If you were to use cards to keep names, addresses and other relevant information about individuals or companies, you would undoubtedly organise each record card so that the information it contained is displayed in a consistent way – so that you know exactly where to look on the card for the particular item of information you require. In a simple index card system for keeping details of family and friends, for example, each individual record card may be arranged like this:

```
NAME:.........................
PHONE NUMBER:.................
BIRTHDAY:.....................
WEDDING ANNIVERSARY:..........
ADDRESS:......................
 .............................
```

Fig 1.1 A simple index card record.

Each of these 'lines' is called, in computer terminology, a *field*. On cards, you could add other fields to some of the records, if you wanted, to meet particular needs. However, generally speaking every record in a computer file must have exactly the same number of fields, even if one (or more) of the individual fields has no information recorded against it.

Just as you can determine what fields you will have on each record of a card index system, so you can determine what fields each record will have when you prepare your own computer files. Also, just as you can have several card-index boxes using the same individual record format, so you can have several computer files using the same field format, and managed by the same file-handling system.

How Organiser separates fields

On the index card record shown in Fig 1.1, each field is written on a separate line. You could, of course, have two fields on one line – the Birthdate and Wedding Anniversary date could be on just one line, for example. Visually, the fields are separated by their names, so as far as you are concerned, putting more than one on a line doesn't matter.

If the fields weren't named, however, you would have to devise another way to identify each field. You would probably use a system in which, for example, the top line will always be the name, the next line will always be the phone number, and so on. In effect, this is what you have to do when you create your own filing system on Organiser: you have to decide the order of the fields in the record, and you have to stick to that order for *every* record in that file.

How does Organiser know where one field stops and another starts? When a record is saved to memory, each field is terminated by a special character – the 'non-printing' ASCII character 9. This is also known as the 'tab' character, since on printers and so on it produces a 'jump' of a set number of spaces along a line, to the next 'tabulation mark'.

When a record is displayed on the Organiser screen, each field is shown on just one line: if there are more than 16 characters in the field, then, when that line is selected (using the cursor keys), it will scroll across the screen, so that you can read it all.

You don't have to worry about how Organiser separates each of the fields in your records – unless, by some flukey playing around, you include a character 9 as one of the items of information within a field. (If you do, then the field will terminate at that character - and the rest of the line will appear as the next field. This can create all kinds of problem).

Organiser's built-in filing system

With the 'filing system' built into Organiser - the one you use for the main menu FIND and SAVE operations – you choose a new line to enter data in a record by using the 'down' cursor key. Organiser places the field terminator at the end of the old line, so that when you recall the record, each line will be displayed exactly as you wrote it.

The 'Main' file thus lets you write the entire record in 'one go'. Every line in the main file is of the same 'type' – a string – and you can have a maximum of 16 lines and 254 characters (a character is any letter, number, symbol or space). You can therefore arrange each record so that the information - as shown if Fig. 1.1 - is on a separate line. Each line is a field - and since you can have any number of lines up to 16 in a record, the Main file in effect has a flexible or variable number of fields - all of them of the string type.

When Organiser obeys a FIND command, it searches through an entire record, not just a part of it. So if you keep birth dates in a similar format – '10/May/60' for example – you could find all friends and relatives with birthdays in May by simply entering '/May' as the search clue. (Entering

'May' on its own could also find Auntie May, and someone living in Mayfield Avenue!).

Organiser's built-in Main file is, therefore, extremely powerful for general purposes. However, when you wish to operate on the information contained within specific fields, it can be a disadvantage that there is not a 'fixed' number of fields – the number can vary from record to record in the Main file, remember. It is also a disadvantage to have all of the fields as 'string' types – which can store letters as well as numbers. Organiser cannot perform mathematical operations on string fields directly: they have to be converted to a numeric form that Organiser can understand first. So if there are to be any mathematical operations on a field (such as adding together monetary values), it is better that the field is defined as a numeric field at the outset, capable of storing numbers only.

The need for a file-handling program

Take a file containing details of Club Members, each paying fees depending on their category of membership – Full, Part-time, and Junior. One of the items of information contained in a record could be the membership category. If you used the built-in Main file and you wanted to know the total income due from 'Full' members, you would have to check through each record, identify and count the 'Full' members, and then multiply the number so obtained by the relevant fee. Using the built-in file, this would mean giving the Full membership information as the search clue, then repeatedly pressing the **EXE** key and counting the number of keypresses to obtain the required number, and finally multiplying that number by the fee. This process would then have to be repeated for each of the other membership categories.

By creating your own Club Membership program and Club Membership file (rather than use the 'Main' file), you can place the class of membership into its own field, and Organiser can be told, by a short procedure, to look at that field for each record and to total the number of members in each category: the same procedure could also evaluate the total fees due from each of the member categories, and display the answer. The answer would be available within one or two seconds – with considerably less effort, and without errors.

This is, of course, a very simple example of the benefits of creating your own file-handling program. The important thing to remember is that, if you need to operate on a series of records, extracting information and making calculations, you will gain considerably by creating a file-handling program. If you don't need to operate on the data contained within a record – but merely need to find the information based on any criteria, then the built-in system is perfect.

A file handling program can be written to analyse the built-in 'Main' file. However, there can be only one 'Main' file at each of the memory locations (RAM or Datapaks), and it is highly unlikely that you will want to use that file for just one purpose only. This means you will find it difficult, if not impossible, to ensure that each record has exactly the same number of lines, and that each line carries the same type of information fairly essential features for a successful 'file-handling' program. This makes the 'Main' file impractical for use with your own file-handling programs: it is better that your programs create new files, with records designed exactly as you want them. Amongst other things, this makes your files easier to use, 'process' and analyse.

Where to keep your files

If you use Datapaks with your Organiser, one of the most important aspects to consider is where you are going to store the file information. If the information in a file is going to change frequently, for whatever reason, then keeping the file on a Datapak can consume storage space at an alarming rate.

The reason is that, when information is changed in a record kept on a Datapak, the old information is not overwritten. Instead a completely new record, containing the unchanged and the updated information, is added to the end of the file, and the original record is 'locked from view'. The process can be likened to using a notebook to write out the records. Making a change to details in one record means crossing out the entire record, and re-writing the record on a clean page at the end of all the other records. Eventually the notebook will be filled up with crossed-out records and 'good' records.

As you will appreciate, even with the large capacity Datapaks, it will not be long before all available space has been used, even though the 'live' or latest, most up-to-date records occupy only a fraction of the total space. It would then be necessary to transfer the file - possibly to a new Datapak - and to re-format the original so that it can be used again. (A Psion Formatter is available for this purpose). If this procedure is acceptable, then Datapaks provide the best, most permanent way to keep files.

Two alternatives are available. The first is to use the internal 'RAM' of your Organiser (location 'A:'), which will limit the space available for your Diary and so on, and the second is to use a Rampack. Rampacks store information more or less the same way as information is stored in the internal RAM of Organiser, and those currently available have a capacity of approximately 32,000 characters. They incorporate a battery with a life estimated at around five years.

The advantage of using RAM or a Rampack to store files is that, when a record is updated, the memory used by the original record is released for re-use: with the card index box analogy, the original record card is removed from the box, and the new record is added, so there is still the same amount of space left in the box.

The disadvantage of using Organiser's internal RAM is that the information could be lost: removing the battery from Organiser for a few minutes, for example, will mean a complete loss of all the information held in RAM. Rampacks have the disadvantage of a limited life (albeit, five years). There are, therefore, pros and cons for each method of storage, and the method you choose depends on your own requirements and the ancillary items you have available.

The ideal solution for those fortunate enough to have access to a PC would be to maintain files in RAM or on a Rampack, and to regularly copy them to PC disks using the Psion Comms link. That way you will have a permanent 'back-up' for your files, while maximising the space available 'on board' your Organiser.

Where to keep your programs

The file-handling programs can of course be kept on Datapaks once they have been tested and proved. You should always enter and develop programs in RAM, and copy them to Datapaks only when you know they are working perfectly to your complete satisfaction: changing programs on a Datapak is like amending records – the entire program is re-written, and the original is 'locked up'.

Also, once you have the program working satisfactorily, you *could* transfer just the *object* code to a Datapak - that is, the part that Organiser uses to obey your instructions - and so save considerable space. The *source* code – which is the instructions you write using Organiser's programming language, is not needed by Organiser once it has been converted to the *object* code. You, however, will need the source code to make changes to your programs: you cannot change the *object* code directly.

Again, the ideal solution is to save your source code onto PC disks using Psion Comms Link, so that you can call them back should it ever become necessary.

Developing programs on a PC

Having mentioned the ideal situation of using a PC as a means of backing up Organiser files and programs, it should perhaps be mentioned that Psion has produced software that will enable you to create (or enter) programs on a PC, and to 'download' them once they have been tested and proved. Called the 'Psion Organiser Developer', this software has many advantages over creating programs on the Organiser itself – not least of which is the large keyboard!

The Developer emulates practically all of the functions of Organiser II (not just the programming facilities). It provides a 'boxed' display on the PC screen which simulates Organiser's screen and shows the effects of running programs on Organiser. The programs themselves, however, are written using the larger screen area of the PC, so that much more of the program can be seen at a time. The Developer also has powerful 'debugging' facilities, which allow programs to be run step by step, variables analysed and so on, making the whole process of creating programs much easier. It also enables complete 'Datapaks' to be 'created' and downloaded into Organiser Datapaks.

The only programs that cannot be run (sensibly) on the Developer are those which 'peek' and 'poke' around in Organiser's memory or which use machine code, for obvious reasons. There are one or two other minor 'restrictions': Organiser's top slot is not recognised by the emulator, and the KSTAT command doesn't effect the PC keyboard when testing a program on the PC.

Needless to say, virtually all of the programs appearing in this book were developed and de-bugged using the PC Developer. They were downloaded into an Organiser, to prove that they worked. Then they were re-loaded back into the word-processor without change. So in theory, they should all work perfectly...

1.2 Planning the Program

The first steps

There are three stages to handling your own files on the Organiser II:

1. Create the file-handling program.
2. Create the file(s).
3. Use the program to perform the necessary file-handling tasks.

If you use Organiser's built-in filing system, stages 1 and 2 have already been done for you: all you have to do is enter and perhaps change the data (stage 3). The FIND and SAVE menu options are effectively commands from the built-in file handling program, allowing you to add, change and delete records, and to search for particular records on any criteria you choose. Organiser creates just one file in RAM, and one on each Datapak or Rampack: as mentioned before, in each case this file is called 'Main'.

To handle your own files, you have to create the specific file-handling program only once. Having done that, (and proved it works) you can then create as many files using that program as you wish – provided you have incorporated 'file creation' procedures in the program, of course! You will give each file so created a different name, so that you can identify the one you wish to use. For example, say that you use the 'Stock Control/Price List' program discussed later in this book. Once the program has been entered, you can have as many separate Price List files as you want – perhaps one for products, one for spares, one for items you have to purchase yourself, and so on. You could also keep a separate Price List file for each month if you so desired. Each file would have its own name.

How do you tell Organiser which file you wish to use? Consider the card-index boxes again. To select a box for use, you would simply 'open it up' so that the record cards are accessible. Strange as it may sound, you have to do the same thing with the particular computer file you wish to use - you have to open it. This action – performed by a special instruction in Organiser's programming language – tells Organiser to select and prepare the particular file for use.

As you will see later on, you can 'open' four files at a time on Organiser, but only one of them can be worked on at a time, and you have to tell Organiser which one that is. (Don't panic - it's not as complicated as it sounds!).

The one file-handling program should be designed to look after all of the files it creates (stage 3). If you additionally want a program that will handle a different type of file – your accounts, for example – then you will need to create a separate file-handling program.

Everyone has their own requirements not just for the types of file they want to keep, but also for they way that they wish to manage those files. Some concepts are common to practically every type of file-handling program (the three stages given above, for example), and it is these concepts that are discussed in this part of the book: an understanding of the concepts involved will help you to adapt the basic procedures, routines and programs given later to your own specific needs. Thus, although we will develop only two complete file-handling programs – for looking after a Stock Control/Price List and for handling a Bank Account – by understanding the processes used to create the various procedures, and by understanding the programs themselves, you should be able to adapt them to provide any other file-handling program you want.

What do you want to do?

The first step when writing any program is to set down exactly what the program is required to do. To demonstrate this, let us take as an example the Stock Control/Price List file handling program. The information we expect to get from the file may be as follows:

1. The item name (and stock number, perhaps).
2. How many (or much) of each item is in stock.
3. Which items need to be re-ordered because stock is getting low.
4. The price of each item (with or without VAT).
5. The stock value of each item.
6. The total value of all the stock.

This is the basic information the file must yield: you may have additional requirements for such a program, such as the source of the stock for re-ordering. You may also have access to a printer, and consequently want to be able to print out the information. Whatever you want your program to do, make sure it's in the list.

In addition to what you want to get out of the file, the file handling program must allow you to perform a number of other tasks:

7 Add new items to the file.
8 Delete items from the file.
9 Change the information contained in each record (in the current example - update the stock-holding, the price, the re-ordering level, perhaps even the item name or reference).
10 Create a new file of data.

These are fairly standard requirements for any file handling program. It all looks pretty obvious when set down on paper doesn't it? Nevertheless, it is well worthwhile taking time to put everything down: if you know all that the program has to achieve, you can plan it properly. It's always easier to write your program to do everything that you want at the outset, than it is to tack bits on afterwards.

The next step is examine just what each record must contain in order to provide the information that is required from the file. In other words, what fields must each record in the file have. Remember, even if we don't use every field for every record, it must still be available to every record. The objective here is to keep the individual records as short as possible – that is, with no more fields than are necessary.

Taking the current Stock Control/Price List example, it would seem that the requirements 1 to 6 given earlier will each need a field on the record. However, requirements 5 and 6 - the value of each item held in stock and the total value of all the stock - can be obtained by calculation whenever they are needed: the value of a stock item is simply the price of the item multiplied by the quantity in stock. The total value is the sum of all of these values. For this example, therefore, we need just four fields:

a) The item name (and possibly its reference number).
b) The quantity in stock.
c) The price of each item.
d) The minimum level of stock.

Map out the program

We are now in a position to see exactly what the program has to contain:

- A routine to create new files.
- A routine to open a specific file.
- Routines to add, delete, and modify records.
- Routines to extract the information required, and possibly to print the information as well as display it.

You'll find that practically every file-handling program will need the basic elements just given, in one form or another, and so they give you a good starting point for your own programs.

Knowing what fields each record in the file must have, and what routines we need to handle our files, we are in an excellent position to start planning and writing the program.

1.3 Handling Organiser Files

Creating and opening a file

Before you can work with a file, it has to be *created*. Organiser has to be told the name of the file you want, and it has to be told where you want the file kept – in RAM ('A:') or on a Datapak ('B:' or 'C:'). This has to be done just once: after that, you have only to *open* the file.

When you create a file, Organiser stores its name in memory, at the specified location, together with a 'reference number' unique to that file's name. This reference number lies in the range 145 to 254 inclusive (in hexadecimal, 91H to FEH). Thus, you can create only 110 files of your own at each location (more than enough!). As a matter of interest, your Organiser uses other lower reference numbers for its own purposes – 144, for example, is used for the file called 'Main', and 131 is used to identify an OPL procedure.

Later, when you add records to the file, each of the records will also be identified by the file's reference number. The point is that when a record is saved to memory, Organiser places it in the next available free space. So, if you have several files in memory, the records for each will be 'mixed up' with each other, along with program procedures and so on. In other words, the records for one specific file are not necessarily stored in consecutive locations in memory: Organiser II knows which records are associated with each specific file by the unique reference number.

How does Organiser know where one record stops and another starts? Each record also contains information about its length – a number from 1 to 254 (in hexadecimal, 1 to FEH). These numbers – the file reference and the length – are each stored in one byte or memory cell, hence every record has an overhead of two memory cells. The length information comes first followed by the file's identifying reference number. The end of all the stored data is identified by the hexadecimal number FF (255), which is the largest number that can be stored in one memory cell. The largest number available, therefore, to show the length of a record is 254, which is one reason why no record can be more than 254 memory cells in length, or 254 characters or bytes.

All this is fairly academic: you don't have to worry at all about the reference numbers, where your records are actually located in memory, or how they are stored. Organiser sorts it all out for you.

When you create a file, Organiser assumes that you will want to use it straight away. It therefore also *opens* the file. When a file is created or opened, Organiser needs to be told the fields you wish to use in the file, and, since you can work on four files at a time, it needs to know which of the four this one is to be.

The fields determine how each complete record is going to be saved or recalled: you will remember that each field is separated from the next in the record by a special character – the 'tab' character, which is a '9' in ASCII.

It is important that you specify the same number and type of fields when you open a file for use as when you created the file, and that you do not use the tab character in your records (CHR$(9)). Otherwise your records will yield errors. This is because Organiser doesn't keep a 'permanent' record of the fields associated with a file, but rather sets up the fields on a temporary basis when the file is opened or created.

The four files that can be worked with at a time are identified by a single letter, from A to D. In your Organiser manual, these are referred to as the logical file name, and they provide a short, easy way to identify which of the four you wish to use for a specific operation.

The OPL words for creating or opening a file are CREATE and OPEN, and the format is as follows:

```
CREATE filename,logical
filename,field1,field2...field16

OPEN   filename,logical
filename,field1,field2...field16
```

Notice how, apart from the OPL instruction, the format for each is the same. CREATE, remember, records the file name in memory (as long as it doesn't already exist), while OPEN searches for the file name in memory and 'makes a note' of the associated reference number (as long as the file name exists) so that it can find the file's records.

Let us examine the commands bit by bit. The *filename* must start with an identification of the place where the file records are stored, as follows:

A: Organiser's built in RAM.
B: A Datapak in the top slot.
C: A Datapak in the bottom slot.

So, if you wish to create your file on the Datapak in the top slot (location 'B'), the filename must start with 'B:'.

The actual name of the file must be no more than eight characters long. It must start with a letter, and as a general principle, it should contain only letters and, if you wish, numerals 0 to 9. (Organiser will 'reject' filenames it doesn't like!). It doesn't matter whether you use capital letters or lower case letters – in a filename, they are the same. Thus B:MYFILE and B:Myfile both refer to the same file.

The logical filename must be one of the letters, A, B, C.or D. It doesn't matter which, so long as you stick to the same letter whenever you refer to that particular file and its records in your subsequent file-handling program (more about this later). Again, you can use a capital letter or a lower case letter, it doesn't matter.

The names you give to fields have to obey the same rules as variable names:

1. Integer fields must end with '%'. (Integers are whole numbers only with no decimal points anywhere in the number).
2. String fields must end with '$'. Unlike string variables, you don't have to specify how many characters will be in the string. (Strings are sequences of any characters - letters, numbers and symbols).
3. Floating point numbers have no terminating symbol.
4. The total length of the field name, including the type identifier (% or $), must not be more than eight characters.
5. The field name must have only letters and numbers, apart from the type identifier at the end.

(Please refer to your Organiser manual, or to '*Using and Programming the Psion Organiser II*' if you wish to know more about variables).

You can have any number of fields, up to a maximum of 16.

When a file is created or opened, an area is allocated temporarily in RAM to hold the relevant field information. If four files are opened (with logical filenames of A, B, C and D), then four areas are created in RAM to hold the relevant field information for each of the four files.

Note that with earlier versions of Organiser, the end of the RAM area when a file is created sometimes needs to be identified. To achieve this, a program must assign a dummy value to the *last* named field, and the entire record added to the file. Since you won't want a dummy record in your file, it can be erased immediately.

Thus, a typical set of 'create' instructions could be:

```
CREATE A:TESTFILE,A,FIELD1,FIELD2,FIELDEND
FIELDEND=0
APPEND
ERASE
```

It must be pointed out again that this dummy assignment, appending and erasing process is required only on some earlier versions of Organiser, and is given in this book to avoid the possibility of errors occurring after file creation. On later models, you can omit the assignment, append and erase instructions without trouble.

Generally speaking, each file handling program that you write will require its own type of file records, with a specific number and types of field. For this reason, it is usually necessary to write a separate 'create or open' segment for each type of file-handling program.

Also, with some kinds of file-handling program, you will only ever want one file. The name of the file can, in such a case, be entered as part of the program and, since you will only need to create the file once, the create routine can be a separate procedure which, once run, can be erased. Here is an example of such a procedure to create a simple, single file called 'A:EXPENSE' in RAM :

```
MAKEFILE:
CREATE "A:EXPENSE",A,DETAIL$,AMOUNT,DATE$
DATE$=""
APPEND
ERASE
```

As mentioned earlier, you may choose to ignore the last three lines. Once run, this procedure could be erased if you wish - the file that you need to use to store the expense records will have been created. (In this instance, in Organiser's RAM).

The file-handling program, or at least the main part of it, will have to open the A:EXPENSE file with exactly the same types of field, although you could if you wish change the actual names of the fields. Thus you could open the file with an instruction in your file-handling program as follows:

```
OPEN "A:EXPENSE",A,INFO$,SPENT,WHEN$
```

The important points to note are that the types of each field are the same when the file is opened as when the file was created (in this case, string, float, string) and that the name of the file, 'A:EXPENSE', is the same. When you refer to the field names in your program, they must be the same as those used when the file was opened, of course: in this case, A.INFO$, A.SPENT, and A.WHEN$. (The 'A.' part tells Organiser that you're referring to the file opened as logical file 'A' – see 'Adding Records'). However, when opening a file it is better practice (and less confusing!) to stick to the field names you used when the file was created.

In the programs given later in this book, it is assumed that you will want to have more than one file – perhaps, in the example just given, you would want an expense account file for each month. Consequently the programs allow the user to create and use (almost) as many files as required. A 'utility' routine is developed to enable a file name to be entered from the keyboard and checked that it is in the correct format.

Adding records

Without exception, it will be necessary for your file-handling program to be able to add records, and in all but a very few instances, it will also need to be able to delete records. The OPL word used for adding a record is APPEND, and for deleting a record it's ERASE.

To add a record using the APPEND instruction, you must assign a value to each of the field variables. Those fields that do not have a value assigned will be given a 'null' or zero value. A field is identified by the logical file name – a letter from A to D – followed by a full point and the name that you gave to the field when you created or opened the file. Thus, if you opened a file with the logical file name of 'A', a string field that you called 'FIRST$' would be identified as A.FIRST$. You assign a value to it in the same way that you assign a value to any variable using OPL. One way would be:

```
A.FIRST$="This is a field record"
```

However, in most instances, you will want to input the information from the keyboard. You can do this with an instruction such as:

```
INPUT A.FIRST$
```

When you assign values to field variables, Organiser stores the information in the area it set aside for the fields of the appropriate logical file: hence the importance of identifying which logical file is being referred to. When all (or as many) of the fields have been assigned with the information you wish to be stored in the record, you simply give the OPL instruction APPEND. On meeting this command when a program is running, Organiser transfers the information temporarily stored in the area set aside for the field information to the appropriate memory pack location. A typical sequence of instructions for adding a record could be:

```
INPUT A.FIRST$       :REM Get a string input
INPUT A.INTEGER%     :REM Get an integer input
INPUT A.FLOAT        :REM Get a float input
APPEND              :REM Add record to the file
```

However, when using the program, you would not find this sequence to be very satisfactory: you would most likely forget what you are supposed to be entering at the keyboard. You would want to give yourself a 'clue' to the information you need to input. This could be done using the PRINT instruction. Thus:

```
PRINT "Enter NAME"
INPUT A.FIRST$
```

If you also wish to prevent the vertical 'scrolling' as each new line is entered onto the screen, you could precede these two instructions with a CLS (CLear Screen) instruction or an AT 1,1 instruction, which positions the cursor in the top left hand corner. (Note that it is not necessary to use AT 1,2 before the INPUT instruction, since the cursor will automatically jump to the next line after the PRINT instruction, provided it isn't followed by a comma or a semi-colon).

In the Utility functions given later in this book, you'll find a routine 'GI$:(*message$,type*)' which will allow you to have a message of any length rolling along the top line, with your input (which can be a string, an integer or a floating-point variable, as determined by *type*) being entered on the second line. This utility makes the display of a message and entering information a simple one-line affair in your program, and makes for a better display. It also means that your message needn't be restricted to 16 characters.

The other aspect to consider, having entered a record, is that you may well wish to enter another one immediately. This can be achieved by enclosing the input sequence of instructions within a loop. One typical loop could be as follows:

```
DO
....
.... all the input instructions
....
APPEND
UNTIL MENU("MORE,END")<>1
```

This particular loop doesn't require any 'Local' variables to control it, and is economical on space. The MENU function returns either a '0' (if the **CLEAR/ON** key is pressed), 1 (if 'MORE' is selected), or 2 (if 'END' is selected). The UNTIL test ensures that the instructions in the loop are repeated every time 'MORE' is selected: when MENU returns 0 or 2, the 'UNTIL...<>1' (not equal to 1) is true, and program processing continues with the next instruction.

Changing records

With most (if not all) file-handling programs, you will want the means to change some of the information held in a record. To do this, it will be necessary to

1. Open the file.
2. Find the record (and view it).
3. Identify the field(s) to be amended.
4. Make the change(s).
5. Re-save the record.

Obvious? Perhaps. But setting it down makes it quite clear what has to be done. In most file-handling programs – and certainly those in this book – the first step will have been done right at the beginning: the file will have been opened for business as the first step.

Find the record

The next step is to locate the record that needs changing. There are two ways to go about this: you can arrange the program to step through every record in the file until the required record is found, or you can arrange for a search clue to be given for the required record. OPL has a number of words to perform these operations:

```
FIRST, NEXT, BACK, LAST, POS, POSITION, FIND.
```

Most of these words are self explanatory: FIRST, for example, selects the first record in the active file, NEXT selects the next record, and so on. POS returns the record number of the current record in the file, while the instruction POSITION x makes record number 'x' the current record. The file-handling programs in this book incorporate both methods – stepping through each record in a file, and searching for a match to a clue – in order to provide complete flexibility of application.

Integral with locating a record is displaying it on the screen, and as you know (or guessed), OPL has several ways of doing this. You can either simply display a suitable field, using for example the VIEW instruction, or you can display the entire record using the DISP instruction.

The format for the VIEW instruction is

```
VIEW(line%,string$)
```

Line% must be either a '1' or a '2', for the top or bottom line of the screen respectively, and string$ is the string variable or information to be displayed. Thus, to display the field 'A.FIRST' on the top line of the screen, the instruction would be

```
VIEW(1,A.FIRST$)
```

The string A.FIRST$ will be displayed on the screen and Organiser will wait until a key - any key - is pressed before processing continues with the next instruction in the program. Organiser 'remembers' this key as an ASCII number and, if you wish, you can assign it to a variable. Thus

```
K%=VIEW(1,A.FIRST$)
```

With this instruction, the ASCII value of whatever key was pressed to allow Organiser to continue obeying program instructions is stored in K%. So if 'A' is pressed, K% will be given the ASCII value of 'A', which is 65. This facility can be useful if you wish your program to act on the key pressed. Consider the following, for example:

```
....
KSTAT 1
LOOK::
K%=VIEW(1,"AMEND "+A.FIRST$+" (Y OR N)")
```

```
IF K%=%Y
....
.... do the Amending routine
....
ELSEIF K%<>%N
GOTO LOOK::
ENDIF
....
.... find another record or finish
```

In this program segment concept, the VIEW instruction displays the contents of the field 'A.FIRST$' sandwiched between 'AMEND' and '(Y OR N)'. The user is being invited to press 'Y' to amend the record, 'N' to continue. If any other key is pressed, a jump is made back to the label 'LOOK::'. Note the easy way of identifying the ASCII value for 'Y' and 'N' – %Y and %N respectively.

This is just one example of how a record can be identified for amendment. You could have any field of a record displayed with the VIEW function, but it is important to remember that the second argument must be a string. So if you wish to display a numeric field, it must be converted to a string first, or converted within the VIEW instruction itself. For example, to display the field 'A.SPENT', which is a float type of field, we could use OPL's FIX$ function as follows:

```
K%=VIEW(1,FIX$(A.SPENT,2,8))
```

The information in A.SPENT is restricted to two decimal places, and the value is converted to a string with a maximum of eight characters, including the decimal point, by the FIX$ instruction. In this form, it can be displayed using the VIEW function. You can, of course, build up a string message – by concatenating – as in the previous example. (Further discussion on the OPL words for converting numeric values to strings is not within the scope of this book: please refer to your Organiser manual).

Viewing an entire record

You may wish to view an entire record, before deciding whether or not you wish to amend (or delete) it. (You will probably also want to view the entire record as part of your file-handling operation). Does this mean a separate VIEW statement for each field? No. There is an OPL function - DISP - which will display all of the current record. This function can be used in three different ways: to display a record that has been selected and made 'current', the format is

```
DISP(-1,"")
```

As with VIEW, Organiser waits until a key is pressed before proceeding with the next instruction: the ASCII value of the pressed key can be assigned to an integer variable.

The slight snag with the DISP function is that it although it displays all the fields, each on its own line, it doesn't state what the fields are. In many instances, this won't matter, but if you have records with several numeric fields, all you'll see is a series of numbers, each on its own line, and you'll have to remember what they refer to. If you wish to have the name of the field on display (or any other descriptive message), you can build up one complete string which combines each of the field values (converted first to strings) along with an identifying message, and separated by the 'tab' character ASCII 9. This string can be displayed, as a complete record, using DISP as follows:

```
DISP(1,string$)
```

To demonstrate how the string can be built up, take as an example just two fields, 'A.STOCK%' and 'A.PRICE'. The program segment could be on the following lines:

```
....
S$="STOCK: "+NUM$(A.STOCK%,8)+CHR$(9)
S$=S$+"PRICE: "+FIX$(A.PRICE,2,8)
DISP(1,S$)
....
```

Notice the use of the tab character to separate the fields. This technique provides a clear display of a record, thus:

```
STOCK: 23
PRICE: 14.23
```

rather than

```
23
14.23
```

The programs developed in this book use the 'captioning' technique to display an entire record.
If the viewing routines are written as a separate function, they can be called not just when you wish to amend or delete a record, but also when you wish to examine the contents in the normal course of events.

Identify the fields to amend

Having located the record to be amended, the next step is to identify which field or fields you wish to change. You could arrange the program so that the entire record is re-entered, but this could be tedious if only a small change is required. In any event, if you wished to change information in all of the fields of a record, it would be just as easy to delete the record and add a new one: in the end the effect would be exactly the same.

Probably the easiest way to select field(s) is to use the MENU function. The MENU list would, of course, be your own guide to the fields. It would be practical to place the MENU function in a loop, so that more than one field can be changed without having to go through the whole process of selecting the 'amend' routine from a main menu for each field. A typical program segment could be as follows:

```
...
DO
C%=MENU("DETAILS,AMOUNT,DATE,END")
IF C%=1
....
.... Edit the 'Details' field
....
ELSEIF C%=2
....
.... Edit the 'Amount' field
....
ELSEIF C%=3
....
.... Edit the 'Date' field
....
ELSE C%=0
ENDIF
UNTIL C%=0
....
```

This loop is fairly self-explanatory: if 'END' is selected from the menu, C% is assigned the value 4, then re-assigned the value '0' by the `ELSE` statement. '0' will be assigned to C% by the Organiser if the **CLEAR/ON** key is pressed while the menu is being displayed. Hence, the loop will allow changes to be made until it is deliberately terminated.

You may wonder why the 'END' option is included in the menu string: why not just use the **CLEAR/ON** key method of exiting the loop? It would certainly cut programming space - since the menu string would be shorter, and the '`ELSE c%=0`' line would not be required. The answer is - there is no strong reason: indeed, if you are sure you will always remember how to exit the loop, then the 'END' option is quite superfluous. But for those occasions when a program is used by other people, or after a long lapse (long enough to 'forget' what you're supposed to do next), you can't beat spelling it out!

Make the change(s)

Having identified the record and the field to be changed, the next step your program must tackle is the re-entry of information. Naturally, OPL has an instruction that allows you to do this - `EDIT`. The format is

```
EDIT string$
```

Notice that `EDIT` requires a string argument. That means in order to edit a number, it must first be converted to a string, using one of OPL's various 'number-to-string conversion' functions (`FIX$()`, `GEN$()`, `NUM$()`, and `SCI$()`). Also, where numbers are concerned, a check should be made that the edited string contains only valid number characters – that is, 0 to 9, '-' and, in the case of floating point numbers, a decimal point – before it is re-converted back to a numeric value.

Thus, the process to edit a numeric value would be

a) Convert the number to a string.
b) Edit the string.
c) Check the string is a valid number.
d) Convert the string back to a numeric value.

One could write a short(ish) procedure to check that a string contains only acceptable numeric characters. Here is a typical example:

```
CHKS%:(S$)
LOCAL C%,V%
C%=1
IF LEN(S$)=0
  RETURN 0
ENDIF
WHILE C%<=LEN(S$)
 V%=ASC(MID$(S$,C%,1))
 IF(V%=%.)OR  (V%=%-) OR ((V%>47) AND (V%<48))
  C%=C%+1
ELSE
RETURN 0
 ENDIF
ENDWH
RETURN 1
```

The string to be checked is passed to the procedure within brackets - thus CHKS%:("123a.4") or CHKS%(N$). Each character in the string is checked until one is found that is not equal to '.', '-', or to one of the digits 0 to 9. In this circumstance, the procedure returns '0'. If all is well, then the procedure returns a 1, so a simple test on the return value can ascertain whether or not the string contains a pure numeric value - for example "IF CHKS%:(1234)" will be 'true' since CHKS% will return a '1'

This kind of procedure could be used to check for any characters in a given string. However, there is a neater and shorter way to check whether strings contain only a numeric value – and that is to rely on Organiser to use its own error-checking routines. If step (c) in the editing process (given a few paragraphs earlier) is ignored, an error will occur if an attempt is made to convert a non-numeric string to a number. This error can be trapped by using the ONERR instruction. Here is a typical example of the last part of an 'Edit' procedure:

```
...
AG::
KSTAT 3
EDIT I$
KSTAT 1
ONERR NN::
RETURN VAL(I$)

NN::
```

(continues overleaf)

```
ONERR OFF
CLS
PRINT "NUMBERS ONLY..."
GET
GOTO AG::
```

The number to be edited is converted (before this procedure segment) to the string I$. The KSTAT3 instruction sets the keyboard to numeric values, to reduce the chance of non-numeric characters being entered. Once the edit has been done the keyboard is reset to capital letters.

Then comes the error-trapping part of the procedure: the ONERR NN:: instruction tells Organiser that if it encounters an error it must jump to the instructions following the label NN::. The next instruction (RETURN VAL(I$)) tells Organiser to return the value of the string I$. If a non-numeric character is present in the string, then normally VAL(I$) would produce a **STR TO NUM ERR**, but since errors are being trapped at this point, a jump is made to NN::. The error trapping is switched off and the message 'NUMBERS ONLY' is displayed (to remind the user that other characters aren't allowed), and a jump is made back so that the string can be re-edited.

One may now ask "Supposing an integer number is edited so that it contains a decimal point?". This won't be found by the error-trapping routine. However, by assigning the returned value to an integer type of variable, the value will be 'truncated' automatically to an integer value, and the decimal point and all that follows it will be lost. This simple technique is usually adequate. However, a different kind of error can occur with integer numbers. As you are probably aware, on Organiser (and most computers) integer numbers must lie within the range -32768 to +32767. If a number outside this range is assigned to an integer variable, Organiser will stop running the program with an **INTEGER OVERFLOW** error message. This can be trapped using the ONERR technique within an *integer* editing procedure. This process is demonstrated in the Utility procedure 'EI%' given later in this book.

Re-save the record

Once the required changes have been made to the selected fields, all that remains is to re-save the entire record. This is achieved with the OPL instruction UPDATE. This instruction writes a completely new record to the file, using the information currently held in all of the field name variables (the unchanged fields and the edited fields). The original record is deleted from the file.

It is quite important to be aware of this operation: it means that the order of the records in the file will change every time a record is updated in any way.

Supposing, for example, that a file contains records in the following order:

RECORD 1
RECORD 2
RECORD 3
RECORD 4

and that RECORD 2 is amended. After the amendments have been made, and the record re-saved (using UPDATE), the order of records in the file will be changed:

RECORD 1
RECORD 3
RECORD 4
RECORD 2

Normally the order of records doesn't make an iota of difference: the Organiser can find any specific record instantly. Remember, too, that a record deleted from a Datapak is in effect only 'crossed out' – it is 'tagged' so that Organiser will ignore it, but it still occupies memory space. In Organiser's RAM or on a Rampak, however, the space occupied by the record is released for further use. Consequently if records are going to be changed frequently (as may be the case with a Stock control file or a Price list), the record files are probably best kept in RAM or on a Rampack.

It is useful to contain the entire record-amending sequence within a loop, so that amendments can be made to several records without having to continually select 'AMEND' (for example) from a main menu. The 'AMEND' sequence could look something like this:

```
....
DO
.... find the record
.... identify the fields to change (a loop)
.... make the change
UPDATE
UNTIL ("ANOTHER,END")<>1
....
```

As you might imagine, this can result in a very long procedure - which would be difficult to follow and to 'de-bug'. It is therefore advisable to break the program up into smaller procedures, which are 'called' as and when required: remember that variables can be made 'global' and that information can be passed to and received from a called procedure.

Deleting a record

The process for deleting a record from a file is fairly straightforward:

a) Open the file.
b) Find the record.
c) Double-check it is to be deleted.
d) Delete it.

The first step, opening the file, will usually have been done at the outset. The next step, finding the record, has already been discussed under 'Changing the Record'. Indeed, if this operation has already been written as a separate procedure (or a set of procedures), all that is necessary here is to call that procedure. That's why it makes sense to break a program down into lots of small procedures.

Once the record has been found, it will be current, ready for further work. In this instance, the further work is potentially to delete it.

The next step is to double check that the record is to be deleted: it is very easy to remove a record in error by careless key-tapping. It is not so easy to restore a record. Once the deletion is confirmed, the OPL word for removing the record is ERASE.

A typical delete sequence could be as follows.

```
.... Find the record
....
KSTAT 1
DL::
C%=VIEW(1,"DELETE "+A.Strfield$+" - Y or N")
IF C%=%Y
  ERASE
ELSEIF C%<>%N
  GOTO DL::
ENDIF
```

The KSTAT 1 instruction sets the keyboard for capital letters. The string displayed by the VIEW instruction is a concatenation (an adding together) to enclose a string field from your file (represented here by 'A.Strfield$') within the message 'DELETE... Y or N'. If 'Y' is pressed, then the deletion is made. If 'N' is pressed, processing continues without the deletion being made. Any other key causes a jump back to the label DL::.

Analysing records

Being able to add, view, amend and delete records really only covers the basic operations of file handling. For a simple file such as an address list, these operations could well be enough. But the chances are you will want your program to do far more. If you have a Stock Control file, for example, you may wish to know the current value of the entire stock being held. Or you may wish to know which items need re-ordering, 'at a glance'.

Most analytical requirements involve the examination of each of the file records in turn, or at least selected fields of each record, and acting on the information found. Provided the precise requirements are known, Organiser can be programmed to do the analysis for you. A simple 'loop' in which this can be achieved might be as follows:

```
....
FIRST
DO
....
.... examine a field
.... act according to its contents
....
NEXT
UNTIL EOF
```

The FIRST instruction makes sure that the first record on the file is the current record. Then comes the loop, where the required field or fields are examined to see whether or not the required conditions are met, or to make the required calculations. To get the total value of stock being held, for example, the field containing the number of items would be multiplied by the cost per item, and the result added into a running total. To see whether an item needed to be re-ordered, a 'current stock level' field would be compared with a 'minimum stock level' field and, if lower, the fact that the item needs re-ordering would be displayed.

Once a record has been 'processed', the NEXT instruction moves the file pointer onto the next record, and the whole process is repeated until the end of the file is reached.

In the case of the 'total values' analysis, the running total would then be displayed, along with any message you deemed suitable.

The benefit of having specific fields to a file should now be even more apparent: accessing numeric values within Organiser's built-in 'Main' file is not an easy task, which makes any form of numeric analysis on 'Main' extremely difficult.

Generally speaking, it is advisable to keep any analytical routines as separate procedures, and to call them from the program's main controlling menu. In this way, it would be easy(er) to write a procedure to perform a once-only task as and when it may be required. The procedure containing the main controlling menu would then be amended to include the new procedure as one of the options.

Using more than one file

For most file handling programs, it will probably be sufficient to use just one file to meet the requirements. There may be occasions, however, when to perform the tasks you want you will need two or more files open at a time. One example of this is contained in this book – a 'Banking' program. In this program, one file is used to record every transaction – cheques paid out, cheques paid in, standing orders, and so on – and the other file is used to store information about the standing orders. Using this technique, Organiser can be programmed to examine the standing order file whenever the program is used, and to automatically 'pay' any standing orders that may be due (by creating a new 'transaction' record), so that the bank balance 'held' in the Organiser is always accurate and up-to-date.

It is important when you have two or more files open at a time that any procedures operating on the files correctly identify the file to be used, and that the correct record is made current. The appropriate file can be selected with the OPL word USE. A common mistake is to think that, because a file has just been used in one procedure, the USE instruction needn't be used in another procedure called immediately after. Your program may call on the second procedure from yet another procedure elsewhere, after another file had been made current.

Similarly, it would be wrong to think that if record four (say) were current when a file was last used, it would necessarily be current on return to that file. Other routines may have changed it. The safe way to avoid hidden problems is to ensure that, each time it is necessary to call a file, that file is made current by the USE command, and that the correct record in that file is selected and made current.

When a file has been made current and a record has been selected, the field information for that record is contained in the temporary area of RAM set aside by Organiser. That information is still available if another file is opened and made current, and a record in that file selected: the field information for the second file is also held in the temporary area of RAM, separate from the information for the first file.
This means once specific records have been selected, information can be passed between them. The assignment of a value held in one field variable to a field variable of a different file takes the expected format:

```
A.file1=B.file2
```

The A and B parts of the field variables identify the logical file names you gave to the files when you opened or created them, not to RAM or slot locations. As with any variables, the types (integer, float or string) must be the same, unless you specifically want to force a float to an integer:

```
A.file1%=B.file2
```

In this instance, the float value held in variable 'B.file2' will be converted to an integer value for storing in A.file1%. The original float value will, of course, still be held in B.file2.

As with any variables, mathematical operations can also be performed using field variables.

It must be remembered that any changes made to a field will not be 'permanent' – that is, recorded back into the file itself – until an UPDATE or an APPEND command is given. If it is required to save the information from both sets of field variables, the two files must each be made current in turn. A typical sequence of events may therefore involve a program embracing the following types of instruction:

```
....
OPEN "A.STOCK",A,ITEM$,QUANT%,PRICE
OPEN "A.PROFIT",B,GROUP$,MARKUP
USE A
....  select a record from file A
USE B
....  select a record from file B
COST=A.PRICE*A.QUANT%
RETAIL=COST*B.MARKUP
```

```
A.QUANT%=0
B.MARKUP=B.MARKUP*.75
....
USE B
UPDATE
USE A
UPDATE
....
```

This is an example of segments from a complete program - which would normally comprise a host of separate procedures. The action of this example is to open a stock file (A.STOCK) as logical file 'A', and a 'mark-up' file (A.PROFIT) as logical file B: both files are held in RAM (determined by the 'A.' part of each file name). The STOCK file is then selected by the USE A instruction to locate a particular item, and the PROFIT file is selected (USE B) to find the 'mark-up' category (we're assuming that items have different degrees of mark-up for the purposes of this exercise). Then come the calculations to evaluate the cost price of the item for the quantity held, and to evaluate the 'retail' price. The quantity is reduced to zero (they've just been sold), and just for demonstration purposes, the markup is reduced to 75% of its original value. The important point to note is that before each record is re-saved, the appropriate file is made current.

Organiser allows you to have up to four files open at a time, but do remember that only one of them is current at a time for input and output operations.

That concludes our introduction to the theory of file-handling. We will now develop some utility routines, to help make the task of writing file-handling programs easier.

CHAPTER 2

File Handling Utilities

2.1 Adding To The Language

Who needs more functions?

Since Organiser's programming language OPL already contains a very extensive range of commands and functions, you may wonder why one would want to extend it further. The fact of the matter is, OPL has been specifically devised to enable you to 'add' to the functions it provides to make your own life easier when writing programs. This is one of the beauties of OPL.

The functions described in this Chapter enable a program to be broken down into smaller segments. This action can enable longer programs to run on Organiser. The reason lies in the way Organiser runs a program. Briefly, what happens is this.

When you 'run' a program, either from the PROGram menu or from the main menu, Organiser loads the object code for the program into its RAM area. Control of the Organiser is then passed to the program, and the instructions it contains are obeyed. If the program is all in one – that is, just one procedure – the whole program will be loaded into RAM. If however the program comprises a number of routines or functions which it 'calls' as required, the shorter, main part of the program is loaded into RAM, and the individual functions are loaded only as and when they're needed.

The point is that when the instructions in a separate procedure are completed, that procedure is effectively 'removed' from memory, releasing the space for another to be loaded when required. If a routine is 'called' 30 times by the main program, it will be loaded and 'cleared' 30 times from RAM memory. If the same routine were written 'in-line' – that is, written out in full in the main program wherever it is needed, it would require 30 times more memory space than the separate routine.

It is therefore advantageous in terms of memory alone to break a program down into discrete parts: a program that takes up more than 24kbytes of memory (and stored on a Datapak) can, if carefully planned, run on a 16k or even an 8k machine. Question: doesn't all the loading and clearing of separate functions make the operation of the program slower? Answer: yes. But we're talking here of thousandths of a second: you will rarely, if ever, spot the difference.

There are other benefits to building a program from short routines and functions. It is far easier to test that a short routine works properly. Also, once a routine has been written and tested, it can be used in any program. You won't have to write that routine again.

So, in this Part of the book, we are going to develop a few routines which will add some handy functions for use in other programs, particularly file handling programs.

The routines given here can be adapted and changed to suit your own requirements, of course. They can also give you ideas for creating your own functions. However, it must be pointed out that most of the routines given here are used in the programs given later, and so all the inputs and outputs to these routines must be retained if you intend to enter the other programs. So that you can fully understand the routines and make use of them in your own programs, each is described under headings as follows:

What it does

Under this heading, you'll find a discussion of the purpose of the routine – why it is useful, what it does in detail, perhaps how 'calling' it can save time and/or space in other programs.

Space required

It can be useful to know just how much space a procedure or a complete program is going to take up in your Organiser or on a Datapak. There are three ways to save a procedure:

a) Before it is TRANSlated. When saved this way – usually during the development of a procedure or when a break is made during entering the entire routine – only the source code is saved. That's the 'code' that you actually enter, the OPL commands and statements.

b) After it has been TRANSlated. When saved this way, both the source code and the object code are saved. The object code is the one Organiser actually uses when it 'runs' the procedure. Both source code and object code are saved together under the one 'heading' – the name you give to the procedure. Organiser knows where one stops and the other starts, so you don't have to worry about it.

c) When copying the procedure to another location. If 'OBJECT ONLY' is selected then only the object code is saved at the new location. This means that the source code is missing from the procedure (at the new location), so it occupies less space, but you will be unable to make changes to the procedure at that location. You are advised, therefore to 'back up' your routines or to copy source and object code if you think you may wish to adapt or change them at a later date.

Whichever way you save a procedure, there is an 'overhead' of some 15 bytes, used by Organiser to 'organise' itself.

Under the heading 'Space required' you'll find an evaluation of how much space is occupied by the procedure:

a) By the object code with the overhead
b) By the object code and the source code, with the overhead.

But please note that the figures given are for procedures as written but *without* all the leading spaces shown in the listings, and *without* any of the REMarks that may be included. The leading spaces are included in the listings to help you to identify the matching IF...ENDIF, DO...UNTIL and WHILE...ENDWH sections of the code. They are not required for the procedures to run, and they are unnecessarily space consuming.

It should also be pointed out that the space figures quoted are for guidance only: they have been derived by examination of the procedure in Organiser's memory. Obviously any changes you make to a procedure will affect the space requirement.

How it works

So that you can understand better the concepts used when developing a procedure, a description of how it works is given. In some instances, the operation of the procedure will be fairly self explanatory – and easy to understand from the description given under the heading 'What it does'. In these circumstances, only the briefest description is given.

Examples of use

One or more examples of how the routine is 'called' by other programs is given, so that you will be able to understand how to use it in your own programs.

Inputs and Returns

As previously mentioned, many of the routines given in this section of the book are used by the two main file-handling programs: should you choose to modify the routines to suit your own requirements, it is important that the input requirements and the type of information returned is exactly as given under these headings.

Non-OPL functions called

In some instances, the routines will themselves 'call' other routines – the whole secret of structured programming, remember, is to break the programs up into the smallest possible chunks. Under this heading will be given the names of the other non-OPL functions that are called: these functions must be entered into the Organiser for the routine being detailed to operate.

Globals needed

It is often handy to have Global variables in a program - that is, variables that can be used by any procedure called after the variable has been 'declared'. One such variable, for example, could be used to 'hold' the question-mark symbol '?': it is easier to write – and remember – say 'Q$' than CHR$(63). Also, sometimes it can be more suitable to use Global variables which can be accessed directly by all procedures and routines, rather than using Local variables and passing information back and forth to other procedures by arguments and return values. If a routine needs Global variables to have been declared before it is called, you will be told so under this heading. The Global variables listed must, of course, be declared in a program calling the routine.

Variables used

In order to keep the source code for the procedures as short as possible, abbreviated rather than explicit variable names have been used: thus S$ rather than STRING$. This is fine for saving space (to say nothing of the time and effort taken to enter a procedure into Organiser), but can make some procedures and routines very difficult to follow. For example, in a program listing, it would be easier to understand

```
TOTALSUM=UNITCOST*QUANTITY
```

than

```
T=U*Q
```

However, the explicit version is nearly two dozen characters longer, and that's in just one line of code. Also there are less chances to make mistakes when entering the shortened variable names, and for these reasons, abbreviated variable names have been used. Under this heading you will find details of what the variable names used in the procedure stand for, or their purpose.

You will find that some variable names – C%, for example – are used by a number of procedures. This causes no problems provided that they are Local variables: the Local variables used in one procedure are quite independent of Local variables used in other procedures, remember, so they can have the same name.

Customizing

In a number of instances, you may well prefer that a function handles things somewhat differently to the way it is written here. Under this heading you'll find some general notes on how the function can be customized to suit your own purposes. However, do remember that the types of input and return values should be retained if you intend to enter any programs in this book that call the procedure you customize.

The Listing

This is the routine that you will enter into your Organiser (or modify, as the case may be). Please note the following points:

1. Program lines are indented for loops and IF type instructions, to make it easier for you to understand the operation of the program. The leading spaces do not have to be entered. However, if you are new to programming, you may find it better to enter the leading spaces initially and to test that the procedure works without errors: the spaces can help you to locate missing ENDIF or ENDWH statements. Once the program TRANslates and runs satisfactorily, the spaces can be deleted and the program re-saved, to minimise the space required.

2. The :REM construction is used occasionally to help explain the purpose of a particular line in the procedure. This too can be ignored: it plays no part whatsoever in the running of the program, and will only take up unnecessary space.

3. The procedures have all been downloaded from an Organiser, without any change whatsoever: if a procedure doesn't run or you get error messages during the TRANslation process, please check your entry against the listing very carefully, paying particular attention to variable names, and make sure you have included all the other procedures that are necessary for the program's operation.

Test program

By their very nature, most of the functions are not 'stand-alone' programs. In other words, you will have to test them by calling them from another program: often this is best achieved by writing a simple test routine that can be erased once all is known to be well. Using this method, you will know that the component 'parts' of a larger program work as planned, and you shouldn't have to search through all the individual procedures and functions to find the 'bugs'. Where practical, a typical Test Program is given.

2.2 How To Enter a Program

The Basic Principles

This short section is for those who have yet to experience the joys of entering a program and who may therefore be a little uncertain or hesitant about how to go about it. The programming menu (selected by choosing PROG from the menu that appears when the Organiser is first switched on) offers a number of options:

```
EDIT LIST DIR
NEW RUN ERASE
COPY
```

These options are described in this Chapter to guide the newcomer through all the processes involved in entering, editing and manipulating program procedures and functions.

NEW
(To enter a new routine)

This is the option you will choose when you first enter a new procedure or function – that is, one that you haven't entered either in full or in part before. When the option is selected, the screen display will clear and the word NEW will appear followed by a letter denoting the location Organiser proposes to eventually save the routine that you enter. Thus 'NEW A:' denotes that your routine will be saved at location 'A', Organiser's built-in RAM. Repeatedly pressing the **MODE** key will cycle the 'save' location through RAM and Datapaks B and C, always provided that Datapaks are fitted to the upper and lower slots, of course.

When entering and editing programs, it is strongly recommended that you select either the 'A' location or, if you have a RAMpack, the location at which the RAMpack is fitted. Saving routines to a Datapak during their development can use up the potential space available on the Datapak very quickly. Once a routine has been written, thoroughly tested and proved, it can be copied or re-saved to a Datapak, should you so wish, thus making it 'more' permanent.

Your first entry, after the prompt 'NEW A:' must be the name of the routine that *precedes* the colon only: if the routine is a function that has brackets following it, you do not enter the colon or bracket part of the name at this stage. Thus, if the function is called 'MSG:(string$)', after the 'NEW A:' prompt you enter 'MSG' and then press the **EXE** key. (Organiser won't let you enter more than eight characters – the maximum allowed in a function or procedure name – and if you do happen to enter the colon and bracket part by mistake, Organiser will tell you that you have a BAD PROC NAME). If the name you enter already exists, Organiser will tell you with the message

```
FILE EXISTS
press space key
```

Pressing the space key will return you to the PROG menu. You will then have to either select NEW again, this time choosing another name, or select EDIT to edit the previously entered routine. Having entered an acceptable name, press the **EXE** key and the screen will clear and then display the name of your routine, followed by a colon. This is the point where you enter the bracket part of the routine, if there is one, followed by pressing the **EXE** key: using the current 'MSG' example, you would enter '(string$)' and press **EXE** .

Thus, to make this as clear as possible, let us go through the sequence to enter the new routine called 'MSG:(string$)' again. First you select the NEW option from the PROGramming menu. Organiser will then display:

```
NEW A:
```

(the location letter may be B: or C:, depending on how Organiser has been used previously). You select the appropriate location by pressing the **MODE** key, then enter the first part of the routine's name, 'MSG':

```
NEW A:MSG
```

You then press **EXE**. (Note that you will get an opportunity to change the location where the procedure is saved when you actually save it).

Organiser will now display the name of your procedure:

```
MSG:
```

This is the point where you must enter the 'bracket' part of the procedure (if there is one) as shown in bold below

```
MSG:(string$)
```

followed by **EXE** again. If there is no bracket part to the name of the routine you are about to enter, you simply press the **EXE** key. Either way, the 'cursor' – or flashing symbol – will move to the extreme left of the second line, ready for you to enter the program.

You can now enter your routine, line by line. At the end of each line, you press the **EXE** key – just as you would press the carriage return key on a typewriter. The cursor, which indicates where your next entry will be, will move to the start of the next line.

While entering a routine, you can use the 'arrow' keys to move the cursor up or down or along any of the lines entered so far, and you can use the **DEL**ete key to remove the character to the left of the cursor, or the **SHIFT** and **DEL**ete keys together to remove the character at the cursor position. Pressing the **CLEAR/ON** key will clear everything entered on the current line or, if the line is blank, it will remove the line completely. You can thus clear any mistakes you may have made, and re-enter the correct information.

As mentioned previously, the listings in this book use leading spaces on some lines to help make routines easier to understand: you do not have to enter these leading spaces. Nor do you have to enter '`:REM`' or anything that follows it on a line: `REM` stands for 'remark', and is used only to help in understanding how a routine works.

When you have completely entered the routine, or if you wish to stop entering the routine for the time being, press the **MODE** key. The screen will clear, and you will be presented with a further 'mini' menu with three options.

```
TRAN SAVE QUIT
```

The options offered by this menu are as follows.

TRAN This option should be selected only if you have finished entering all of the routine. It tells Organiser to 'translate' the lines of 'source' code that you have entered into a different kind of code (called 'object' code), which Organiser uses to actually run the procedure. If there are any mistakes in the way that you have entered the code, Organiser will tell you with an 'error' message: you'll find an explanation of these messages in your handbook. In most cases, when you press the keys as instructed by the messages, you will be returned to a point in the procedure where Organiser believes you have made the mistake. The error(s) must be put right before the routine can be translated and used.

After a *successful* TRANslation, the screen will clear and the word SAVE followed by the location letter and the procedure name will be displayed. If you wish to change the location, you can use the **MODE** key, as before. When you are happy that the correct location has been selected, press **EXE**, and both the 'source' code and the 'object' code for the routine will be saved.

SAVE If you have entered only part of a routine and wish to take a break, simply select the SAVE option: the 'source' code you have entered will be saved, as it stands, for further development at a later time. The routine will not be translated into the 'object' code that Organiser uses when running programs, and therefore it cannot be used yet.

QUIT If you wish to abandon what you are doing, select this option: everything that you have entered *during the current session* will be lost. This option is most often selected when you 'edit' a previously entered routine, and are just looking through it without making any changes, or if you make changes that you decide to abandon. The original routine, as previously saved, will still be in memory.

EDIT
(To change or inspect a routine)

You should choose this option from the PROGramming menu when you wish to make changes to the 'source' code of a routine, or when you just want to inspect it. The screen will clear and display 'EDIT A:'. You use the **MODE** key to select the location where the routine was saved, and enter only the name part of the routine, *not* the colon or any 'bracket' part. Provided that you have correctly selected the location where the routine can be found, and provided you have also entered its name correctly, the screen will again clear and the start of your routine will be displayed. You can then use the 'arrow' keys to move around the routine, editing it as you choose. (See also under 'NEW').

When you have finished editing, press the **MODE** key, and the 'TRAN, SAVE, QUIT' menu will appear: you now have the option of (re)translating the source code into object code (TRAN option), of simply saving the source code for further development later on (SAVE option), or of abandoning any changes that may have been made to the source code during the current session (QUIT option).

It is worth repeating that you are strongly advised to save the routines you edit in Organiser's RAM ('A:') or on a RAMpack until you have thoroughly tested and proved them, and you are absolutely sure you do not wish to make further changes.

RUN
(To run a translated procedure)

This option enables you to 'run' a translated program, provided it isn't a function. Functions are those procedures which need an input 'argument', indicated by a bracketed part following the name (as in 'MSG:(string$)' for example). When RUN is selected, the screen will clear and the word RUN followed by a location letter will be displayed: you enter *just* the name of the program or procedure you wish to run, and use the **MODE** key to select the location at which it has been saved.

Note that the program you run can 'call' procedures and functions at other locations: Organiser will search through *all* of the available memory to find them.

If there are any 'run-time' errors in a procedure, or in any of the procedures that make up a complete program, Organiser will stop running to report the error, and will give you the option of editing the offending routine in order to correct it. The most common errors you'll come across are MISSING EXTERNAL and MISSING PROC

MISSING EXTERNAL means the procedure has a variable name in it that Organiser cannot find among any of the 'Local' or 'Global' declarations. Organiser will display the name of the 'external' it cannot find on the second line of the screen. Pressing the **SPACE** key will reveal the name of the procedure where the error occured: this could be the routine you named when you selected 'RUN', or it could be one of the procedures called by that routine. Pressing the **SPACE** key again will give you the option of editing the offending procedure: if you select 'Yes', then the procedure will be listed in the 'Edit' mode, and in most instances, the cursor will be positioned at the point where Organiser spotted the error.

The chances are you have mis-spelt the variable name when entering it, or the variable has an incorrect 'type' identifier, or it is not meant to be a variable at all but a *procedure* name that is missing the 'colon'. Check spellings carefully. Check that it has been declared as a 'Local' variable. Alternatively, if the variable is one known to be 'Global' (that is, declared in a calling routine rather than the routine in which the error has occured), check that the calling routine is present in Organiser.

MISSING PROC means a procedure has been called which Organiser cannot find anywhere. The *name* of the missing procedure will be displayed on the second line of the screen. Pressing the **SPACE** key reveals the name of the *procedure* in which the error occured, and pressing it again gives you the option to edit that procedure.

Check that you have spelt the name of the procedure correctly (with the identifying tag), and that the procedure has been entered, translated and saved satisfactorily. If the procedure is on a Datapak, check that the Datapak has in fact been plugged into the Organiser!

For details of all the error messages, please refer to your handbook, or 'Using and Programming the Psion Organiser II'.

ERASE
(To remove unwanted procedures)

Select this option to remove both the 'object' and the 'source' code of a procedure from memory. As with the NEW and EDIT options, at the prompt you select the location of the procedure using the **MODE** key, and then enter the procedure's name. Organiser will ask you to confirm that you do wish to erase the procedure from memory (just to make sure).

Note that when a procedure has been saved in RAM or on a RAMpack, the space it occupied is released for further use on erasure. The space occupied by procedures on a Datapak is not released for further use on erasure: consequently frequent changes to procedures on a Datapak will soon consume all available memory.

DIR

(To see a list of procedures)

With this option, you can view a list of all the procedures that have been saved at a particular location. Having selected the option, use the **MODE** key to select the location you wish to examine, then press the **EXE** key repeatedly to view the list of procedures. To stop at any time, press the **CLEAR/ON** key. You will be returned to the PROG menu.

COPY

(To copy procedures)

This option enables you to copy procedures from one location to another. The destination location must be different from the source location. When the option is selected, you will be asked whether you wish to copy the object code only: choosing 'Yes' enables you to conserve space when copying a proven routine to a Datapak. However, if you then subsequently erase the procedure at the original location, you will not be able to edit it any further, since the source code must be present for editing purposes.

Note too that the copying process places an extra drain on the battery supply: make sure you have a fresh battery in position before starting, or use the mains lead that is available (a most invaluable optional extra). Once you have ascertained whether or not you wish to copy both source and object code or just the object code, Organiser will display the message 'FROM'. You must then *enter* the location of the procedure from the keyboard (A, B or C) followed by a colon and, for just one procedure, the name of that procedure.

If you wish to copy all of the procedures from one location to another, then the location letter and the colon are all that need be entered at this point.

The screen will then display 'TO', and again you enter the destination location letter followed by a colon. It is not necessary to re-enter the name of the procedure unless you wish to re-name it at the new location. But be careful if you do this, especially if the procedure is one that is called by other procedures – for its name will have to be changed in those too.

Once all has been entered, pressing **EXE** will set the copying process in motion. The time taken to copy from one location to another depends on how much is being copied: you will hear 'clicks' during the copying process. Copying a number of procedures can take a comparatively long time.

LIST
(To list a procedure to a printer)

If you have a printer connected to your Organiser through an RS232 link (or Comms Link), you can choose this option to obtain a print-out of any procedure. Once LIST has been selected, use the **MODE** key to select the location of the procedure if necessary, then enter its name and press **EXE**.

2.3 Briefly Display a Message

MSG:()

What it does

It is often extremely useful to display a message on the screen for a brief period, as a reminder of what to do next, perhaps. This short function does just that: as given here, it clears the screen, provides a short 'bleep', displays the message for a timed period, then gives another short 'bleep' before control is passed back to the calling routine. This reduces the five lines required for the routine to just one in the 'calling' program, and would need to be called only two or three times in a program to make a saving in memory space. It can also make the 'calling' program easier to understand.

Space required

As listed, but without leading spaces or 'REMarks' (see Chapter 2.1).

Source + object code: 113 bytes
Object code only: 58 bytes

How it works

The procedure uses the OPL PRINT statement to display the message, and hence if there are more than 16 characters to the line, the overflow will appear on the second line. If there are more than 32 characters in the message, the top line will dissappear from the screen. The alternative – having the message scrolling on just one line – would entail the use of the VIEW function, which in turn requires a key to be pressed before the message is cleared.

Examples of use

The following three program lines show how the MSG function can be called from a procedure.

```
a)    MSG:("Watch me")
b)    MSG:(M$+N$)
c)    MSG:(M$+"pots"+N$+CHR$(63))
```

Examples b) and c) require that M$ and N$ have been properly declared and assigned a string value, of course (i.e. M$ = "WOW").

Inputs

The message string must be enclosed within the argument brackets in the calling routine. This can be an actual string (example a)), or a combination of one or more string variables (example b)), or a combination of string variables, actual strings and string functions (example c)).

Returns

Nothing.

Other non-OPL functions called

None

Globals needed

None.

Variables used

S$ = String$. This is the procedure's 'argument': it automatically takes the 'value' of the string in the 'calling' instruction, and doesn't need to be declared as a Local variable. It cannot be amended by the MSG:() function.

Customizing

There are many ways this procedure can be adapted to suit your own particular requirements. You can remove completely either or both of the BEEP instructions, or simply change the note or its length. You can alter the display period by changing the value in the PAUSE instruction: the measure is in twentieths of a second, remember, so the delay is currently set at 1 second. If you want a higher delay period, by making the value also negative you can ensure that a key press will terminate the routine. Thus `PAUSE -100` will provide a delay of 5 seconds or until a key is pressed, whichever occurs first.

This procedure is used in File programs listed elsewhere: be careful, therefore, about changing its general structure.

The Listing

```
MSG:(S$)
CLS
BEEP 50,500
PRINT S$
PAUSE 20
BEEP 50,500
```

Test programs

Either (or both) of the following short programs can be entered, translated, saved and run to test the MSG:() function. Once proven, the test program(s) should be erased from memory.

1)

```
TESTMSG:
MSG:("THIS IS A TEST")
```

2)

```
TESTMSG2:
LOCAL M$(16),N$(16)
M$="THE.TOP.LINE...."
N$="THE.BOTTOM.LINE"
MSG:(M$+N$)
```

2.4 Yes or No Test

YORN%:

What it does

One of the most frequent requirements when running an inter-active program is to obtain a 'Yes' or 'No' answer from the keyboard, and to act according to that answer. This short procedure provides a routine that handles the task in a neat way: if the answer is 'Yes', a '1' is returned, while if the answer is 'No', a zero is returned. No other answer is accepted. The calling routine can therefore be as simple as

```
IF YORN%:
...
... do the 'Yes' routine
...
ELSE
...
... do the 'No' routine if required
....
ENDIF
```

As you can see, the complete test is undertaken in the calling program by the one, simple instruction 'IF YORN%:'. The instruction following this statement is obeyed if the statement is true – that is, if YORN%: returns a non-zero result.

Note that two approaches are available should it be necessary to test only for a 'No' answer:

1)

```
IF YORN%:
ELSE
...
... do the 'No' routine
...
ENDIF
```

2)
```
IF YORN%:=0
...
... do the 'No' routine
...
ENDIF
```

In terms of the source code, the second method is slightly shorter, and probably easier to understand.

Space required

As listed, but without leading spaces or 'REMarks' (see Chapter 2.1).

Source + object code: 206 bytes
Object code only: 94 bytes

How it works

The function displays the message on the second line of the screen (always), by using the OPL word VIEW. This allows for a question to be displayed on the top line by the calling program - the message should, of course, be less than 16 characters to avoid scrolling.

VIEW displays the message "(Y)es or (N)o" until a key is pressed. The ASCII value of the pressed key is 'returned': we want to know whether the 'Y' or a 'N' key has been pressed, and so a simple test of whether the returned value is the ASCII for 'Y' or 'N' is peformed.

It is possible that the keyboard may have been set to lower case characters or numerals, and so the KSTAT command is used to make sure the keyboard is first set to capital letters. It would be possible, once the YORN%: routine is running, to over-ride the KSTAT command by pressing (for example) the **SHIFT** and **NUM** keys. No provision is made to trap this type of (rare?) event.

Examples of use

Examples of how this procedure is called from another procedure or function have been outlined in previous paragraphs. Overleaf you will find a summary.

a) *To act on Yes and No answers*
```
CLS
PRINT "query message"
IF YORN%:
....do Yes routine
ELSE
....do No routine
ENDIF
```

b) *To act on a Yes answer only*
```
CLS
PRINT "query message"
IF YORN%:
....do Yes routine
ENDIF
```

c) *To act on a No answer only*
```
CLS
PRINT "query message"
IF YORN%:=0
....do No routine
ENDIF
```

Inputs

None: but it is expected that the top line of the screen will be used to display a message of up to 16 characters (maximum). If between 17 and 32 characters are used, they will be lost on the second line: any more than 32 will cause scrolling.

Returns

1 if the answer is 'Yes'
0 if the answer is 'No'.

Other non-OPL functions called

None

Globals needed

None

Variables used

A% = Answer Used to hold the result of the keypress. Note the use of an integer variable (the identifying '%' symbol).

Customizing

This procedure is used in File programs listed elsewhere: be careful, therefore, about changing its general structure if you wish to enter those programs.

For your own programs, you could re-write the YORN% function, calling it, for example, 'YORNWM%:(M$)', so that it will print the message as well as returning an answer. (The 'WM' in the name stands for 'With Message'). Such a function could be created using the listing given for `YORN%:`, by simply adding the following two lines immediately before the `KSTAT 1` instruction:

```
CLS
PRINT M$
```

It will be necessary when calling the modified routine to place your message (maximum 16 characters) in brackets after the function name thus:

```
IF YORNWM%:("Repeat.test"+CHR$(63))
... do 'Yes' routines
etc.
```

Note that this modification to the routine clears the screen before the message is displayed. It is not used in any of the programs listed later.

The Listing

```
YORN%:
LOCAL A%
KSTAT 1
ST::
A%=VIEW(2,"(Y)es or (N)o")
IF A%=%Y
RETURN 1
ELSEIF A%=%N
  RETURN 0
ENDIF
GOTO ST::
```

Test programs

Here is a simple routine to test YORN%:. To use it (once entered, TRANslated and SAVEd), run the routine twice, first pressing **Y** and then **N** and noting the result: YES or NO should appear at the left of the top line according to the keypress. Note that only the keys **Y** or **N** should have any effect. Press any key to exit the test routine each time. Erase the test routine once you are happy YORN%: works.

```
YTEST:
PRINT "IS THIS O.K"
IF YORN%:
PRINT "YES"
ELSE
  PRINT "NO"
ENDIF
GET
```

2.5 Get an input

GI$:()

What it does

Practically every program requires some kind of keyboard input from the user. We have already dealt with a simple 'Yes or No' type of input, but what about inputs of information? Most programs – particularly those involved in file-handling – require a considerable amount of different kinds of information to be keyed in, and each time it is necessary for the program to print a suitable message, then obtain the input. This function, although it looks fairly long, makes it easy to write the program lines that get information from the keyboard, and of course, it can be used for as many different programs as you wish. In other words, it provides an extremely useful function to add to those already in the OPL language. The function copes with any type of input requirement – floating point, integer or string – and to make it even more useful, it is arranged so that a long (and sensible) message can be displayed to explain what input is required.

Space required

The space required for the procedure, as listed, but without leading spaces or 'REMarks' (see Chapter 2.1) and excluding space required by any of the non-OPL routines called is:
Source + object code: 521 bytes
Object code only: 208 bytes

How it works

When called, the function is given two arguments: the message (M$) related to the required input, and a tag (T%) to identify the type of input being requested. The tag must have a value of 0, 1 or 2, for floating point, integer or string inputs respectively.

The screen is cleared, and the keyboard is set to suit the type of input required – either numbers only or numbers and letters – using the KSTAT command. The message is then displayed on the top line using

OPL's VIEW function, so that messages longer than 16 characters will be scrolled. As you are know, VIEW waits for a key to be pressed before it allows processing to continue with the next instruction. This can present a problem: it means a key has to be pressed before the actual input can be accepted. To get round this, the ASCII value of the pressed key is saved (in C%), and displayed as the first input character at the beginning of the second line (PRINT CHR$(C%);): the semi-colon after this instruction ensures that the rest of the input will be displayed immediately after the first character, so that from a user's point of view, only one input is being made.

The rest of the input is obtained in the usual way using OPL's INPUT command, and then the 'first' character is added to the beginning of it, so that the input string variable represents the total input. There is a minor snag to this technique: all but the very first character can be 'edited' during the input. That is to say, if an error is made during entry, all but the very first character can be corrected in the usual way using the cursor and **DEL**ete key. It is felt, however, that this is preferable to the alternative of having to press a key before making the actual input – which can easily lead to errors and frustration.

Obtaining a single character through the VIEW function enables us to test for an immediate 'abort'. It may be that the user changes his mind about making an input – and simply presses **EXE**. Consequently, immediately following VIEW a simple test is made to see whether the **EXE** key has been pressed (by checking whether the ASCII value of the key-press is 13). If it has been pressed, we need to return a value according to the type of input required: a '0' for integer or floating point requirements, or an empty string for string requirements.

Having obtained the input, we need to test that it conforms exactly to the requirements of the calling program. For example, if a floating point number is required as an input – and the calling program is all geared up to accept a floating point number – it would create an error if anything other that a floating point number is returned. We must therefore test that no alphabetic characters are present in the returned string. We can use the fact that Organiser will detect errors of this kind, by building in an error-trapping routine.

Thus, before the string representing the input is returned to the calling routine, a simple ONERR test is made by extracting temporarily the value of the input according to the calling routine's requirement. If there is an error, processing jumps to the `BN::` labelled part of the function. This displays a message briefly (using the MSG:() function given in this section of the book), before going back to the start to receive a new input. Note that this error-trapping routine will also detect integer values outside the permitted range -32768 to +32767.

You may ask "Why not return the value exactly as requested by the calling routine, instead of a string each time?" The reason is OPL won't let us do that from a single routine: you will recall that when a function returns a value, its name requires an identifier to indicate the type of value being returned: no identifier for floating point numbers, '%' for integer numbers, and '$' for strings. A function can have only one identifier, and while numbers can be represented as strings, strings cannot be represented by numbers (sensibly). Hence, this is a string function. It is up to the calling routine to make the simple conversion required to turn the string into a numeric value.

Please note that no test is made to ensure that the value of T% is within the range 0 to 2: it is encumbent on programmers using the routine for their own purposes to ensure that T% does indeed lie within this range. The additional programming lines required to perform such tests are quite unjustified.

Examples of use

The function can be called by a program to obtain a floating point, integer or string input from the keyboard. Examples of each are given below: note that the message is not restricted to 16 characters, and that the value of the second argument in the brackets is vital to the type of input being requested (see under 'How it works'). Note too that this function returns a string, which must be converted to a number, by the calling program.

a) *Floating point inputs*

Format: `V = VAL(GI$:(M$,0))`

i) `V=VAL(GI$:("Enter the cost",0))`

ii) `V=VAL(GI$:(M$+N$,0))`

b) *Integer inputs*

Format: `V% = VAL(GI$:(M$,1))`

i) `V%=VAL(GI$:("How many books"+CHR$(63),0))`

ii) `V%=VAL(GI$:(M$+N$,1)`

Note that the assignment to an integer variable will force the string's value to an integer, even if a floating point number has been entered.

c) *String inputs*

Format: `V$=GI$:(M$,2)`

i) `V$=GI$("What is your name",2)`

ii) `V$=GI$(M$+CHR$(63),2)`

Note that the string variable being assigned must have been declared with sufficient space to receive the input string (i.e. Local V$(32))

Inputs

Two input arguments are required within the brackets: the request message as a string or string variable, followed by the appropriate tag in the range 0 to 2:

0 = to get a floating point input
1 = to get an integer input
2 = to get a string input

Returns

A string representing the keyboard input. Note that all but the very first character can be edited during input. The calling routine must convert the string to a numeric value, if required.

Non-OPL functions called

MSG:().

Globals needed

None

Variables used

M$ = Message The input string argument.
T% = Tag The input-type identifying tag.
S$ = String Holds the information entered from the keyboard.
C% = Character Holds the ASCII value of the first character input from the keyboard, and used to test for a true integer value.
V = Variable Used to test for a true floating point value.

Customizing

This function is used extensively in the File Handling programs listed later: customization is not recommended.

The Listing

```
GI$:(M$,T%)
LOCAL S$(32),C%,V
ST::
CLS
IF T%=2
  KSTAT 1
ELSE
  KSTAT 3
ENDIF
C%=VIEW(1,M$)
IF C%=13
  IF T%=2
    RETURN ""
  ELSE
    RETURN "0"
  ENDIF
ENDIF
AT 1,2
PRINT CHR$(C%);        :REM NOTE SEMICOLON
INPUT S$
S$=CHR$(C%)+S$
ONERR BN::
IF T%=0
  V=VAL(S$)
ELSEIF T%=1
  C%=VAL(S$)
ENDIF
RETURN S$

BN::
CLS
ONERR OFF
MSG:("BAD NUMBER")
GOTO ST::
```

Test Program

The following routine can be entered to test the three uses of GI$:(). It may seem a little long, but is well worth the effort – and it will help you to understand the function. In use, press any key after each re-display of your inputs. Try entering 'wrong' information, to see what happens. Once all is o.k., erase the routine from memory.

```
TESTGI:
LOCAL F,V%,S$(32)
F=VAL(GI$:("ENTER FLOAT VALUE",0))
V%=VAL(GI$:("ENTER WHOLE NUMBER",1))
S$=GI$:("ENTER YOUR NAME",2)
PRINT "HI THERE"
PRINT S$
GET
PRINT "YOUR FLOAT:"
PRINT F
GET
PRINT "YOUR NUMBER:"
PRINT V%
GET
```

2.6 Get Pack Location

GL$:, UL$:

What they do

When you use Organiser's FIND and SAVE functions (for example), you can select the location – A: (for the internal RAM), B: or C: (for a Datapak) by pressing the **MODE** key. A similar function can be useful for your own programs, particularly as file names must include the location letter and a colon. The two short routines offered here provide a simple way to select the location by pressing the **MODE** key. The first procedure, GL$:, displays a message

```
Pack? Now=A:
```

and accepts presses of the **MODE** key to cycle the location letter through B: and C: (even if Datapaks aren't fitted to the slots!). Any other key-press will return the currently displayed location letter followed by a colon. The routine can therefore be used by the calling routine to complete a file name. The actual work of cycling the location letter is done in the short routine UL$:. Needless to say, both routines must be present in the Organiser: note that, as listed here, both also need Global variables declared in the calling routine.

Space required

The space required for the procedures, as listed, but without leading spaces or 'REMarks' (see Chapter 2.1) is:

GL$: Source + object code: 194 bytes
GL$: Object code only: 95 bytes
UL$: Source + object code: 132 bytes
UL$: Object code only: 80 bytes

How they work

The two routines depend on the calling program declaring a Global integer variable – L% – in order to retain the location information. This information is stored in a simple way: 1 to 3 for the locations A to C respectively. A question mark is used in the GL$: routine, and this too must be declared as a Global and assigned in the calling routine.

The operation of GL$: is fairly straightforward. The screen is cleared and the entire message is displayed on the top line, using the semicolon technique to 'assemble' the various parts of the message. Notice how the last part of this message line (effectively `PRINT UL$:`) calls the `UL$:` routine – to set L% – and prints the return string value. Having set the Global variable L%, all that remains to be done is to return the letter corresponding to its value, which is achieved by simply adding 64 to the value of L% and converting the result to a character.

The `UL$:` procedure may need a little explaining for those not used to programming. Essentially what we need to do is add 1 to L% each time the routine is called (it starts by being initialised to zero). If adding 1 to L% results in its value becoming 3, then we must subtract 2 to cycle it back to 1 again. All this could be achieved by a series of program lines: however, OPL's powerful logical operating system allows us to do the whole thing in one line.

The two tests 'if L% is less than 3' and 'if L% is greater than 2' are performed within the bracket parts of the line. If the first test is 'true', it results in '-1' (Organiser's way of representing 'true') and one is added to L%. Ultimately, adding one to L% will give it the value 3: the first bracketed test will then not be true (resulting in a zero), while the second test will be true, so the bracket part will resolve to -1, and since +2 multiplied by -1 is -2, two will be deducted from the value of L%. Too complicated? Don't worry about it. It works.

Example of use

A procedure using this pair of functions could have the following lines in it:

```
INPUT F$
F$=LEFT$(F$,8)
F$=GL$:+F$
```

This example gets an input (a file name without any location letter), strips it down to eight characters (the maximum allowed in a file name), then tacks on the location letter at the beginning by calling GL$: (note the use of the colon after GL$:. Without it, you will get a MISSING EXTERNAL error).

Inputs

None

Returns

UL$: adjusts the value of L%, and returns L% converted to a location string to GL$:. In turn, GL$: returns a location string to the calling routine.

Non-OPL functions called

GL$: calls UL$: .

Globals needed

Both need L% declared in a calling routine. Additionally, as written here, GL$: needs Q$ to have been declared as a Global and assigned CHR$(63) in a calling routine.

Variables used

None apart from the Globals mentioned above.

Customizing

These routines have been specifically developed for use in the File handling programs given later. They undoubtedly represent just one of many ways to tackle the problem of obtaining a location letter in a cyclic manner. To avoid the dependence of external Global variables, CHR$(63) can be used instead of Q$ in the GL$: procedure.

The Listings

Enter, translate and save the two procedures separately.

a) *The 'Get Location' routine*

```
GL$:
ST::
CLS
PRINT"Pack";Q$," Now=";UL$:
IF GET=2
  GOTO ST::
ENDIF
RETURN CHR$(L%+64)+":"
```

b) *The 'Update Location' routine*

```
UL$:
L%=L%-1*(L%<3)+2*(L%>2)
RETURN CHR$(64+L%)+":"
```

Test Program

Enter the following short routine if you wish to test out the operation of `GL$:` and `UL$:`. When using this routine, enter a name from one to eight characters, then you will be able to select a location (even if you don't have Datapaks fitted) by simply pressing the **MODE** key. You will then be shown the name you entered turned into a file name for the selected location.

```
TESTL:
GLOBAL L%,Q$(1),F$(10)
PRINT "ENTER 8 LETTERS:
INPUT F$
F$=GL$:+F$                    :REM COLON VITAL
PRINT "FILE NAME ="
PRINT F$
GET
```

2.7 Get a File Name
GFN$:()

What it does

File-handling programs will need to operate on at least one data file. The name of the data file could be written into the program as a permanent feature. However, this would obviate the possibility of creating separate, individual files from the program as and when the need arises: you may wish to have a separate 'expenses file' for each month of the year, for example. Entering a file-name on request is a simple enough matter (what could be easier than INPUT F$?).

However, in order to eliminate most, if not all, of the potential errors that can occur (and which would stop the program from running), a number of tests need to be made. If more than one file needs to be called up in a program (or you have more than one file handling program), it makes sense to create a routine specifically to get in the file name and check it out at least for 'syntax'.

This is just such a function. It allows a message to be displayed on the top line to tell the user what input is expected. It checks that a location has been specified: Organiser needs to be told where the file can be found (or where it is to be created). If the location has been missed from the file name, the user is prompted to give a location by simply pressing the **MODE** key, and the location is added to the file name. Finally a check is made to see that the user isn't trying to specify a location which doesn't have a Datapak fitted. (Tut tut!). All these are potential program stoppers if left unchecked.

Space required

The space required for the procedure, as listed, but without leading spaces or 'REMarks' (see Chapter 2.1) and excluding space required by any of the non-OPL routines called:

Source + object code: 464 bytes
Object code only: 207 bytes

How it works

The function uses the utility `GI$:()` to display a helpful message and to get in the actual input. This is tested to see if the user has a colon in the second character position – indicating that a location letter has been entered. If no colon is present, the `GL$:` (and hence `UL$:`) routines are called, and the location added to the file name (having first made sure it is not overlength). Then comes a simple test to see whether the selected location actually exists: an attempt is made to open the 'Main' file at the location. (A 'Main' file is created for you on every Datapak). Any errors that may occur are trapped, and processing jumps back to the start. Otherwise, 'Main' is closed and the accepted file name is passed back to the calling routine.

Examples of use

The returned File-name can be assigned to a string variable, or used in a command, as shown by the following two examples. Notice that the message can be any length (up to 255 characters).

a) `FN$=GFN$:("ENTER THE FILE NAME")`
b) `CREATE GFN$:("ENTER NEW FILE NAME"),A,A$`

Inputs

The message to be displayed must be enclosed within the brackets either as a string or a string variable.

Returns

A File-name, with location identifying letter, scrubbed nice and clean.

Non-OPL functions called

GI$:()
GL$:

Globals needed

None

Variables used

a) *Input argument*
M$ = Message The message input for passing on to GI$:()

b) *Global variables*
  L% = Location Holds the pack location information.
  Q$ = Question Holds the question mark character.

c) *Local variables*
  F$ = Filename Holds the file name in this routine.
  C$ = Check Used to check the location letter.

The Listing

```
GFN$:(M$)
GLOBAL L%,Q$(1)
LOCAL F$(10),C$(1)
Q$=CHR$(63)
ST::
CLS
F$=GI$:(M$,2)
IF MID$(F$,2,1)<>":"
  IF LEN(F$)>8
    F$=LEFT$(F$,8)
  ENDIF
 F$=GL$:+F$
ENDIF
C$=LEFT$(F$,1)
TRAP OPEN C$+":MAIN",A,A$
IF ERR
  MSG:("NO PACK "+C$ )
  GOTO ST::
  ELSE
  CLOSE
ENDIF
RETURN F$
```

Test Program

The following simple routine will test the `GFN$:()` function. When entered, run it several times trying different types of entry.

```
TESTG:
PRINT GFN$:("ENTER A FILE NAME NOW")
GET
```

2.8 Edit Functions

EF:(), EI%:(), ES$:()

What they do

OPL has an instruction 'EDIT' which allows you to edit a string. However, when it comes to file handling, you will undoubtedly wish to edit entries which are also of a numeric nature – and these can be either floating point or integers. It is easy enough to convert such numbers to strings, edit them, and convert them back to the required type. However, the conversions back to a number should be tested to make sure that they still conform to type: if a numeric variable is edited to contain an alphabetic character, a program-stopping error can occur.

Since editing can represent an important and frequently used part of working with files, it makes sense to create the editing facilities as separate functions. At the same time, it is useful (particularly when holding money values) to add in a facility to the floating-point edit function to enable the number of decimal places that will be displayed to be specified.

Space required

The space required for these procedures, as listed, but without leading spaces or 'REMarks' (see Chapter 2.1) and excluding space required by any of the non-OPL routines called, is:

EF: Source + object code: 286 bytes
EF: Object code only: 114 bytes
EI%: Source + object code:173 bytes
EI%: Object code only: 63 bytes
ES$: Source + object code: 110 bytes
ES$: Object code only: 64 bytes

How they work

The floating point function, EF:() requires two inputs: the floating point value to be edited, and the number of decimal places to be displayed. It converts the input value to a string (truncated to the requested number of places) using OPL's FIX$ function, clears the screen, displays an edit message and sets the keyboard for numeric inputs ready for the edit. After editing, the keyboard is set back to alphanumeric inputs, and an 'attempt' made to return the value of the edited input. If there is an error – because a non-numeric character has been included in the edit – the error trapping routine is invoked and processing jumps back to allow the user to re-edit.

The integer editing function, `EI%:()`, takes an integer input and in one short line, attempts to return the integer result of a floating point edit – with no decimal places – by calling `EF:()`. The integer value is converted to a floating point value for `EF:()` using the OPL `INTF()` function. The floating point routine `EF:()` will trap any non-numeric characters: the `EI%:()` routine traps any integers outside of the permitted range -32768 to +32767, giving an appropriate message and allowing a re-edit.

The `ES$:()` function completes the suite and is a straight use of the edit function, with the added flavour of an instructive message. Note that it is necessary to create an independent string: Organiser won't let an input variable be edited.

Examples of use

The most common use for these functions will be to edit the value or data held in an existing variable. Thus:

1) *Declared variables*
   a) `V =EF:(V,2)`
   b) `I%=EI%:(I%)`
   c) `S$=ES$:(S$)`
2) *File field variables*
   a) `A.COST=EF:(A.COST,2)`
   b) `A.QTY%=EI%:(A.QTY%)`
   c) `A.NAME$=ES$:(A.NAME$)`

Notice how only one variable is needed in each case.

Inputs

`EF:(F,D%)` needs a floating point value (F) and an integer value (D%) representing the desired number of displayed decimal places.
`EI%:(I%)` needs an integer value (I%)
`ES$:(S$)` needs a string (S$).
In all instances, the values can be actual values or a variable of the appropriate type.

Returns

The edited input value or string, conforming to input type.

Non-OPL functions called

EI%:() calls EF%:()
MSG:()

= Globals needed

None

Variables used

1) *By EF:()*

V = Variable The floating point input value
N% = Number of decimal places to be displayed
I$ = Input The string of the input value

2) *By EI%:()*

V% = Variable The integer input value

3) *By ES$:()*

S$ = String The input string
I$ = Input String for editing.

Customizing

These functions are used in the File Handling programs listed later.

The Listings

Enter and save the three procedures separately.

1) *Edit a floating point value*

```
EF:(V,N%)
LOCAL I$(12)
I$=FIX$(V,N%,12)
CLS
PRINT "EDIT NUMBER"
AG::
KSTAT 3
EDIT I$
KSTAT 1
```

```
ONERR NN::
RETURN VAL(I$)
NN::
ONERR OFF
CLS
MSG:("NUMBERS ONLY")
GOTO AG::
```

2) *Edit an integer value*

```
EI%:(V%)
AG::
ONERR BI::
RETURN EF:(INTF(V%),0)
BI::
MSG:("NUMBER TOO BIG")
GOTO AG::
```

3) *Edit a string*

```
ES$:(S$)
LOCAL I$(32)
I$=S$
PRINT"EDIT DATA"
EDIT I$
RETURN I$
```

Test Program

The following test program allows you to test all three functions. Run it several times: try entering characters when editing a number, and so on, to see the effects. Clear the test program when all is well.

```
TESTE:
LOCAL V,V%,S$(32)
V=1234.5678
V%=4444
S$="TESTING"
V=EF:(V,1)
V%=EI%:(V%)
S$=ES$:(S$)
PRINT"V NOW",V
GET
PRINT"V% NOW",V%
GET
PRINT"S$ NOW",S$
GET
```

2.9 Show a Record

SR%:()

What it does

When handling files, one of the things you will undoubtedly want to do will be to inspect the individual records. As you would expect, there is an instruction in OPL to handle this requirement – `DISP` – which comes in three 'flavours'. When displaying a complete record using the form `DISP(-1,S$)`, the 'S$' is ignored and the current record is displayed one field to a line. This is fine unless you have several numeric fields and aren't quite sure what each one represents.

The solution is to create a string which adds a name to each field, and separates each name + field part with a 'tab' character – ASCII 9. The version `DISP(1,S$)` can then be used to display the string so produced – S$. Producing such a string must depend entirely on the specific program requirements – and cannot be 'generalised'.

An example of how a string can be produced is given in the routine called '`BREC:`', in the 'BANKER' file handling program. Having created such a string, one could then quite simply use the `DISP()` function as described. However, one will also want to be able to step backwards and forwards through the records of a file. If more than one file is being used (as in the 'BANKER' program given later), it can save space to combine the routines for stepping backwards and fowards together with the record display routines.

The `SR%:()` function does just this: it displays a prepared string, moves to the next selected record and returns the ASCII value of the key pressed so that a new string can be prepared, or the examination sequence terminated.

Space required

The space required for the procedure, as listed, but without leading spaces or 'REMarks' (see Chapter 2.1) is:
Source + object code: 253 bytes
Object code only: 110 bytes

How it works

The listing should be fairly self-explanatory. A string prepared for the current record by the calling routine is passed as an argument to this function, which then sets the keyboard to capital letters (to avoid input problems as far as possible), and displays the string using the DISP() function.

DISP() allows the cursor keys to be used to examine each line of the record. Like VIEW, it requires a character key to be pressed before processing can continue with the next instruction. The key press is used to reset the record pointer as follows:

N selects the next record.
B selects the previous record
F selects the first record
L selects the last record

Note that if the end of the file is reached, the last record is re-displayed. Whatever key is pressed, its ASCII value is returned, so that the calling program can also act accordingly to either terminate record viewing, or prepare a new string for viewing based on the new current record.

Example of use

A typical part of a routine using SR%:() could be as follows. It is assumed that 'S$' is a string prepared from the current record.

```
...
DO
C%=SR%:(S$)
UNTIL (C%=13) OR (C%=%S) OR (C%=1)
...
```

Record viewing will terminate when **EXE**, **CLEAR/ON** or the letter **S** is pressed.

Inputs

The concatenated string, built from names given to record fields and the actual fields, with tab characters separating the name-and-field combinations.

Returns

The ASCII value of a key pressed during the record viewing.

Non-OPL functions called

None

Globals needed

None

Variables used

S$ = String The input string to be displayed.
C% = Check The ASCII value of a pressed key

Customizing

This function is used in the File Handling programs listed later.

The Listing

```
SR%:(S$)
LOCAL C%
KSTAT 1
C%=DISP(1,S$)
IF C%=%N
  NEXT
  IF EOF
    LAST
  ENDIF
ELSEIF C%=%B
  BACK
ELSEIF C%=%F
  FIRST
ELSEIF C%=%L
  LAST
ENDIF
RETURN C%
```

Test Program

The SR$:() function requires a file of records to be present, and necessitates the preparation of a string based on the file's records. A full test program would therefore be extremely long and quite impractical. The following, however, should check the.function works in principle. Notice how the up and down cursor keys allow you to move up and down through your record, and that long lines will scroll under the control of the horizontal cursor keys.

Warning: you will get an error message if you press any of the keys **B, N, L, F,** since these will cause the SR%:() function to try to select a new record in a non-existent file.

```
TESTS:
LOCAL S$(64),C%,T$(1)
T$=CHR$(9)              :REM TAB CHARACTER
S$="NUMBER:"+NUM$(5,2)+T$
S$=S$+"NAME:   "+"JOE BLOGGS"+T$
S$=S$+"HIDDEN: "+"1234"
C%=SR%:(S$)
PRINT"YOU PRESSED",CHR$(C%)
GET
```

2.10 Month Name Selector

MN$:()

What it does

Given a month number as an input, this function returns the first three characters of the month's name. Thus, MN$:(4) will return 'APR'. That's it, folks!

Space required

The space required for the procedure, as listed, but without leading spaces or 'REMarks' (see Chapter 2.1) is:
Source + object code: 160 bytes
Object code only: 87 bytes

How it works

The appropriate mid-section is returned from a prepared string, by multiplying the month number by three (three characters to a name) and subtracting two from the result to get back to the first letter of the name.

Examples of use

a) `M$=MN$:(6)`
b) `PRINT "THIS IS",MN$:(MONTH)`

Inputs

The month number, as a number or an integer variable.

Returns

The first three characters of the month's name.

Non-OPL functions called

None

Globals needed

None

Variables used

M% = Month The input month number

Customizing

The principle behind this one-line function can be used for a variety of similar routines – perhaps to 'decode' file record entries. Your records could have a field which contains a simple numerical integer, for example, which can be expanded by one short routine to give an appropriate name, just as this routine expands a month number into a name. All the 'names' or entries in the string would have to be the same length, of course, but you could use spaces to 'pad out' the shorter names. A considerable saving on file memory space can be achieved by this technique, particularly where standard names are used frequently.

The Listing

```
MN$:(M%)
RETURN MID$("JANFEBMARAPRMAYJUNJUL
(line continued)    AUGSEPOCTNOVDEC",(M%*3)-2,3)
```

Test Program

```
TESTM:
PRINT "IT IS ";MN$:(MONTH)
GET
```

2.11 Truncate a number

DN:()

What it does

This short function trims a floating point number down to a specified number of decimal places. Such facility is useful, for example, for reducing floating point numbers down to two decimal places for monetary displays, and so on. A similar facility – called 'FIX' – is available in the CALCulator mode of Organiser, but this resets the whole Organiser to the required number of decimal places, until it's reset. There is also a 'FIX$' function in Organiser's programming language: to avoid confusion with these two functions, this routine is named 'DN', for 'Decimal Number'.

Space required

The space required for the procedure, as listed, but without leading spaces (see Chapter 2.1) is:
Source + object code: 84 bytes
Object code only: 40 bytes

How it works

Quite simply, the input value is converted to a string 'fixed' to the required number of decimal places, and the resulting value of the string returned. All in one line.

Examples of use

a) `V=DN:(4.2345,2)     :REM V will hold 4.23`
b) `PRINT DN:(V,DP%)`

Inputs

The number to be truncated (V) as a floating point value or a variable, and the required number of decimal places (DP%) as an integer value or variable.

Returns

The pruned foating point value (as a floating point number – not as an integer, even if zero decimal places are requested).

Non-OPL functions called

None

Globals needed

None

Variables used

Input arguments
V = Variable The floating point number to be truncated
DP% = Decimal Places The number of decimal places required in the answer.

The Listing

```
DN:(V,DP%)
RETURN VAL(FIX$(V,DP%,12))
```

Test Program

A test program would be umpteen times longer than the function. You can, however, test it by switching Organiser to the CALCulator mode and entering the function (as shown in bold) in the following example (press **EXE** to get the result). Also use your own values to experiment with the results (note that the 'INT()' is important for entering an integer when using the CALCulator, since in this mode all numbers are otherwise considered to be floating point values):

```
CALC:DN:(1.24789,INT(2))
=1.25
```

2.12 Pad out a String

FIL$:()

What it does

Quite often you will need to space displays out on your Organiser and on a printer, if you have one. Organiser has functions that allow numeric values to be converted to strings – and 'padded' or truncated to a specific length, but there's no similar function for strings. This routine fills the gap (pardon the pun). Alternatively, it can be used to truncate a string to a given length.

Space required

The space required for the procedure, as listed, but without leading spaces or 'REMarks' (see Chapter 2.1) is:
Source + object code: 183 bytes
Object code only: 83 bytes

How it works

First of all a string 'holding' array is declared, and it is assigned a number of characters from the start of the input string, depending on the requested length. If the length of the 'holding' string is equal to the specified length, the result is returned without any more ado. If the 'holding' string is short of the specified length, it is padded out using the OPL `REPT$()` function.

Example of use

If 'S$' holds "This string", then after
a) `S$=FIL$:(S$,4)`, 'S$' will hold 'This',
b) `S$=FIL$:(S$,14)`, 'S$' will hold "This string" followed by four spaces.

Note: The assigned string, (S$ in these examples) must have been declared of sufficient length to accept any extra spaces.

Inputs

The string to be padded or truncated (M$), and the required length for the string (L%).

Returns

The truncated or padded string.

Non-OPL functions called

None.

Globals needed

None.

Variables used

a) *Input arguments*

M$ = Message The input string

L% = Length The required length for the returned string.

b) *Local variables*

S$ = String An array to hold the truncating or padding operation, ready for return (it is not possible to change the input argument, M$, directly).

Customizing

You may like to have a similar routine that pads or truncates at the start, rather than the end. If so, simply use RIGHT$() instead of LEFT$, and add 'S$' at the end of the REPT$() function instead of at the start.

Note that the routine, as listed here, is used in the Stock Control and Banker programs, to create a neat output on a printer.

The Listing

```
FIL$:(M$,L%)
LOCAL S$(36)
S$=LEFT$(M$,L%)
IF LEN(S$)<L%
  S$=S$+REPT$(" ",L%-LEN(S$))
ENDIF
RETURN S$
```

Test Program

The following routine can be entered to test the FIL$:() function. The angled brackets in the VIEW statement will help you to identify the beginning and end of the string – you wouldn't know where the spaces ended otherwise!. Delete the test routine when you're satisfied FIL$:() works.

```
TESTF:
LOCAL S$(32),V%
DO
  PRINT"ENTER STRING"
  INPUT S$
  PRINT"LENGTH"
  INPUT V%
  VIEW(2,">"+FIL$:(S$,V%)+"<")
UNTIL MENU("MORE,END")<>1
```

2.13 What's the Remainder?

MOD:()

What it does

This short routine gives the remainder that's left after one number has been divided by another. It's a function found in many other programming languages – but not in OPL. No problem – we can create it. There are a number of occasions when one wishes to know – or test – the remainder resulting from a division, rather than the actual answer. To give just one example, supposing you wanted to know whether a specific year is a leap year. If it is *exactly* divisible by 4 (or 400, for the 'century years') – so there is no 'remainder' – then as you know, it is a leap year. Thus 1988 divided by four gives no remainder, so it is a leap year. 1989 divided by four gives a remainder of '1', so it isn't a leap year.

This routine makes the test simple by returning just the remainder (or 'modulus') of a division.

Space required

The space required for the procedure, as listed, but without leading spaces or 'REMarks' (see Chapter 2.1) is:
Source + object code: 84 bytes
Object code only: 52 bytes

How it works

Consider how the remainder can be found by taking an example – 17 divided by 5, for instance. 5 'goes into' 17 three times, with a remainder of 2. The remainder can be deduced by multiplying the *whole* part of the answer by the divisor (3 multiplied by 5), and deducting the result from the original number, 17. Thus

17–(3x5) = 2

We can get the *whole* part of the answer by taking the integer of the division, thus

Remainder from 17/5 = 17–(INT(17/5)x5)

This is how the function works.

Examples of use

a) `R=MOD:(21,6)`

b) `R=MOD:(N,D)`

b)
```
IF MOD:(YEAR,4)
  PRINT "NOT A LEAP YEAR"
ENDIF
```

Inputs

Two input arguments are required: the number to be divided (N) and the divisor (D).

Note: *Both of the input arguments must be floating point values.*

Returns

The remainder resulting from the division, as a floating point value.

Non-OPL functions called

None

Globals needed

None

Variables used

Input arguments

N = **Number** The floating point value to be divided.

D = **Divisor** The dividing value (floating point).

Customizing

This routine is called by other programs given in this book.

The Listing

```
MOD:(N,D)
RETURN N-(INT(N/D)*D)
```

Test Program

The easiest way to test this function is in the CALCulator mode of your Organiser. In this mode, enter the function as indicated below in bold, and press EXE. Test the function using your own values.

```
CALC:MOD:(1988,4)
=0
```

CHAPTER 3

Stock Control/Prices Program

3.1 Taking Stock

...or keeping track

The program described in this part of the book has been designed to give you the rudiments of a Stock Control/Price List program. But it could equally well become a Cataloguing program, a Club Membership program, or any similar file-handling program, by suitably adding or changing the fields, and the analytical routines.

The basic elements of a file-handling program were discussed earlier in Chapter1. To refresh your memory (and save you from searching back through the pages), every file-handling program, with few exceptions, must have procedures to:

1. Create a new file and open an existing file.
2. Add new records to the file.
3. Amend existing records in the file.
4. Delete records from the file.
5. Print out the file records.

These procedures give the basic rudiments for handling a straightforward 'data base' of records. However, we can do more than this. We can add analytical routines to provide us with some pretty quick answers to our questions. For example, (as we are looking at a Stock Control program), we can answer questions such as "Which items need re-ordering?", "What is the value of the stock for each item?", "How much VAT has to be added to each item, to the total stock for each item, and to all the stock?" and "What is the total value of the stock held?". No doubt you will have different analytical requirements, but these are the questions our program will answer to show you 'how it is done'.

To give us the required information, each record must contain data as follows:

- The name or identification of the item.
- How many (or much) of the item is held in stock.
- The cost (or selling price) of each item.
- The minimum stock level.

This program assumes we are dealing with specific quantities of items – Gaggle-pin Widgets, Dickery-dock Gaskets, and so on. Equally, though, it could handle weights or volumes. For example, if you wanted a stock control program to handle groceries, you would be more interested in how many pounds of apples you had, rather than how many apples. No problem: the price would be per pound, the stock level and the minimum stock level would be related to the number of pounds, and the pricing would be 'per pound'.

Adapting the program

You may now be asking, how can the program described here be converted to handle your own needs, which may be nothing to do with stock control? Let us look at the possible requirements of a Golf Club Membership list, to demonstrate. First of all, the basic elements (as listed in 1 to 5 at the start of this Chapter) remain unchanged. So the routines given later will provide guidance on how to tackle these elements. The next step is to set down what you want to obtain from each record and from the file as a whole. The list may look like this:

- Member's name, address and telephone number.
- Member's handicap.
- Member's 'category' (and hence annual fee, perhaps)
- List of members who haven't paid their dues.
- Total amount of fees due.
- Total amount of fees outstanding.

And so on. If you compare these requirements with those for the Stock Control program, you'll find similarities – enough, hopefully, for you to be able to adapt the procedures given in this section to a Club Membership program, if that's what you want, and to create any additional requirements you may have. For example, to meet the above requirements, each record could contain the following information (or fields):

- Member's name.
- Member's address and phone number
- Member's handicap
- Membership category
- Paid/not paid indicator.

To find the sum outstanding through unpaid fees, you would write a procedure to check through every 'Paid/not paid indicator' field to identify the members who have not paid: the category field can then be used to obtain the appropriate fee – and that fee added into a grand accumulator, so at the end you will have a figure relating to the fees outstanding.

You would need a routine which (perhaps on a specific date), reversed all of the 'paid-up tags' to 'unpaid tags', and which 'doubled up' on any 'unpaid tags' still remaining, to show that those members 'now' owe two lots of fees.

In the Stock Control program, you'll find a technique for searching through a specific field of all the records and acting according to the information contained each time. In the Banker program given later, you'll find a routine that updates information held in records on a specific 'anniversary'. One of the beauties of Organiser is that it contains a real-time calendar which can be accessed from your programs.

Patently, it is impossible to write a generic program to handle every likely file-handling need. Hopefully, you will get all the information you need to tailor a program to satisfy your own particular requirements by following the methods used in the programs and routines that follow, and by studying the explanations given for each of the individual routines.

Entering the program

All of the routines listed in this Chapter of the book must be entered for the STOCK program to run: you will also have to enter most of the utility functions (listed in Chapter 2) as well. You will notice that some of the utility functions are called by several of the procedures that go to make up the STOCK program: you have only to enter the required utilities once, of course.

The information about each of the procedures that go to make up the entire STOCK program follows the general format for the procedures given in Chapter 2, to help you understand what it's all about.

Note: It is recommended that you enter the routines in Organiser's RAM ('A:') or on a RAMpack during the development, saving them to a Datapak only when you are completely satisfied they work the way you want. It is also recommended that you save the actual files in Organiser's RAM or on a RAMpack.

Space required

Assuming all the routines are entered as listed, but without leading spaces or REMarks (see Chapter 2.1), the total amount of space required for the Stock Control program is as follows

Utility procedures called:
Source + object code: 2652 bytes
Object code only: 1176 bytes

Stock Control procedures
Source + object code: 4748 bytes
Object code only: 2287 bytes

Combined space needed
Source + Object code: 7400 bytes
Object Code only: 3463 bytes

As you can see, there can be a considerable saving in space by copying just the object code of proven procedures, and deleting the 'originals'. But do bear in mind that you cannot edit or change object-code-only routines.

3.2 The main Stock Control routine

STOCK:

What it does

This is the main controlling routine for the entire STOCK program. When run, it asks for the name of the Stock Control/Price list file, automatically requesting the pack location if it is omitted from the name. If it cannot find the file at the specified location, you will be asked whether you wish to create a new file: you may have made a mistake when selecting the location (or simply not fitted the correct Datapak), and so you have the option of saying no – and leaving the program altogether. Otherwise a new file will be created at the specified location.

If the named file is found, it will be 'opened' and you will be presented with a menu of options, from which you make your choice just as you would on the main menu on your Organiser. The options offered by the program are

```
ViewRec Totals
Update AddRec
Printout Del End
```

enabling you to

- View records.
- Obtain Total value of stock, or a list of low-stock items.
- Update a record (i.e. change the field data).
- Add a new record.
- Print out the file.
- Delete a record.
- End the file-handling.

Space required

The space required for the procedure, as listed, but without leading spaces or 'REMarks' (see Chapter 2.1) and excluding space required by any of the non-OPL routines called, is:
Source + object code: 1040 bytes
Object code only: 450 bytes

How it works

The operation of the routine is fairly straightforward, and should be readily understood. Once a file has been opened (by calling on the utility functions of Chapter 2), the routine keeps looping round the MENU, offering the range of options until 'END' is selected or the **CLEAR/ON** key is pressed. When this occurs, the file is closed.

When an option is selected, the appropriate procedure is 'called'. Note that some of the procedures called will themselves call other procedures: all the procedures must be entered for STOCK to run. Note that no error trapping is incorporated for the file creation or file opening segments of the program.

Non-OPL functions called

The following non-OPL procedures are called directly by this procedure. These, and any procedures that they call, must be entered for STOCK to run.

a) *Utilities*
GFN$:()
YORN%:
MSG:()

b) *Stock Control specific routines*
SCFR:
SCTV:
SCUD:
SCANI:
SCPR:
SCDR:

Globals needed

None

Variables used

a) *Field variables*

Note that the variables are given here as they are used when creating or opening a file. When subsequently using the variables for assignments and so on, they must be prefixed by the logical-file letter and a full point. Thus, if the file is opened as logical file 'A', the variable 'I$' is referenced as 'A.I$'.

I$ = Item A string holding the name and/or reference of the stock item.

Q% = Quantity An integer holding the quantity of items in stock.

PE = Price-Each The cost or price of each individual item.

ROL% = Re-Order Level The minimum permitted stock before re-ordering is required.

b) *Global variables*

F$ = Filename The name of the file to be opened or created: this is Global since it is referenced by other routines called by STOCK.

Q$ = Question A handy way to hold the question mark for all the routines in the STOCK suite.

c) *Local variables*

C% = Check Keeps check of the selected option.

Customizing

Customizing the STOCK program has been dealt with in general terms in Chapter 3.1. To give an idea of the scope, field names can be changed - in name and variable type, to suit your own requirements: but be sure to make the same changes to all of the routines that make up the entire STOCK program. For example, if you decide you want another field – perhaps to give the source of the stock item in the record (calling the field 'S$', say), that field must be added to all routines that make use of *all* the field names.

If you wish to add another routine – for a different kind of analysis, perhaps, simply add it into the MENU listing separated by commas and add a 'call' to the procedure handling the selected option, following the style of the other 'calls'. For example, to add an option to show the most expensive stock item – which you might call 'Dearest' – you would add 'Dearest' to the menu list, separated by commas from the other options in the list. If 'Dearest' were the first option (i.e. on selection, C% = 1), then under 'IF C%=1' you would name the procedure performing the analysis. The 'IF C%=x' statements for all the other options would have to be renumbered, of course.

Similarly, if you wish to delete one of the options — 'Printout', for example – simply exclude it from the menu listing, exclude the 'ELSEIF C%=5' instructions (to SCPR:), and renumber 'IF C%=6' to read 'IF C%=5'.

The Listing

```
STOCK:
GLOBAL F$(10),Q$(1)
LOCAL C%
Q$=CHR$(63)
ST::
F$=GFN$:("Stock FileName"+Q$)
IF EXIST (F$)
  OPEN F$,A,I$,Q%,PE,ROL%
ELSE
  CLS
  PRINT "Create New File"
  IF YORN%:=0
    STOP
  ELSE
    CREATE F$,A,I$,Q%,PE,ROL%
    A.ROL%=0     :REM Early Organisers
    APPEND       :REM Early Organisers
    ERASE        :REM Early Organisers
  ENDIF
ENDIF
DO
  C%=MENU("View,Totals,Update,Add,Print,Del,End")
  IF C%=1
    SCFR:
  ELSEIF C%=2
    SCTV:
  ELSEIF C%=3
    SCUD:
  ELSEIF C%=4
    SCANI:
  ELSEIF C%=5
    VIEW("Press a key when Printer ready"
    SCPR:
  ELSEIF C%=6
    SCDR:
  ELSE C%=0
  ENDIF
UNTIL C%=0
CLOSE
```

3.3 Adding a Stock record
SCANI:

What it does

This routine enables a new record to be added to the opened Stock Control/Price List file. Although it is specific to the STOCK program, it demonstrates a process that can be readily adapted to your own requirements. The routine allows any number of new records to be added without returning to the main controlling menu. You can stop entering records by selecting 'END' from the menu given after a record has been entered, or by pressing **EXE** instead of the first piece of information to be entered for the record.

Space required

The space required for the procedure, as listed, but without leading spaces or 'REMarks' (see Chapter 2.1) and excluding space required by any of the non-OPL routines called is:
Source + object code: 535 bytes
Object code only: 278 bytes

How it works

The addition of a new record is controlled within a `DO...UNTIL` loop, enabling you to keep adding records without having to return to the program's main controlling menu each time.

The option not to add any more records is given in the '`UNTIL MENU("MORE,END)<>1`' line: if 'MORE' is selected, a '1' will be returned by the statement and processing will jump back to the '`DO`' statement. Provision is made to cancel the addition of a new record at the start: if the first entry to be made is simply an **EXE**, the `CONTINUE` command causes a return to the controlling program.

Notice how the information for each field is assigned using the GI$:() utility developed in Chapter 2 – and how this utility simplifies the routine.

Notice too that there are no Local (or Global) variables declared in the routine - as you can see, it is not always necessary to assign the result of the MENU function to a variable in order to test it.

Inputs

When creating a routine to suit your own needs, note that the file must have been opened, and the field names must tally with those used when the file was created and opened.

Returns

The routine adds a new record (or records) to the file, based on the latest entered field information.

Non-OPL functions called

GI$:()

Globals needed

As written here, the procedure needs Q$ to have been declared as a Global and assigned CHR$(63) – a question mark – by the calling routine.

Variables used

Field variables

A.I$ = Item A string holding the item name.
A.Q% = Quantity An integer holding the Quantity held in stock.
A.PE = Price-Each A float holding the Price of Each item.
A.ROL% = Re-Order Level An integer holding the minimum permitted stock level.

Customizing

Obviously if you are using this routine as a basis for a routine of your own, you will use the appropriate field names.

The messages to be displayed (through the GI$:() utility function) can of course be anything you wish. But do remember it is better to make the messages clear rather than unduly short.

The Listing

```
SCANI:
DO
  CLS
  A.I$=GI$:("Name of Item"+Q$,2)
  IF A.I$=""
    CONTINUE
  ENDIF
  A.Q%=VAL(GI$:("Current Stock Level"+Q$,1))
  A.PE=VAL(GI$:("Price of each item"+Q$,0))
  A.ROL%=VAL(GI$:("Minimum Stock Level"+Q$,1))
  APPEND
UNTIL MENU("MORE,END")<>1
```

3.4 Find a Stock Record
SCFR:

What it does

This routine allows you to find a record in the opened file in one of two ways – just like FIND on the main menu that appears when you switch on your Organiser.

The first method is to enter a 'search clue', which can be related to any field in a record (for example, you could search for a particular price, if you wished). Repeatedly pressing **EXE** will find all records matching the search clue until the end of the file is met, when the last matching record will be re-displayed. Even though a search clue has been entered, you can still use keys (detailed below) to step backwards and forwards through each record in the file, or to jump to the first or last record in the file. Pressing **EXE** at any time if a search clue has been entered will take you to the next record that matches the clue.

Instead of entering a search clue, you can just press **EXE**, in which case you will be able to step through every record in turn by repeated presses of **EXE**. Keys have also been assigned as below, to enable you to step backwards and forwards:

Pressing...

N will display the next record: if the end of the file is reached, the last record will be displayed.
B will display the previous record.
F will display the first record in the file.
L will display the last record in the file.

In addition, since this routine is also used to locate a record that may need changing or deleting:

S or **CLEAR/ON** will make the record on display the *current* record for further file operations, and return to the calling routine.

Thus two ways to leave the record-examination routine are provided.

When a record is being displayed, the cursor keys (with the little arrows on) will allow you to move around the record to view it all. The information contained in each field of a record is prefixed by an informative 'title': however, please note that this routine controls another routine (SCSEE:) to actually prepare the current record for display. This routine also keeps track of the last matching record in a specified search. The 'SCSEE:' routine uses one of the utilities to actually display the record. Hence three procedures are used to complete the display of a record.

It is important to realise that, if you have amended any records in your file, the order of the records will NOT be the same as the order in which you entered them. This is of no consequence in the majority of instances, since Organiser is capable of finding any record in a flash, if given a clue.

Space required

The space required for the procedure, as listed, but without leading spaces or 'REMarks' (see Chapter 2.1) and excluding space required by any of the non-OPL routines called is:
Source + object code: 728 bytes
Object code only: 329 bytes

How it works

The keyboard is set to receive capital-letter inputs, the very first record in the file is made the current record, and then the utility GI$:() is used to assign a search clue to the variable S$. A message is then given, to remind you of the keys to press, and the 'search' begins using the 'WHILE FIND' technique.

If there is no search clue, this will result in a step through every record each time the **EXE** key is pressed. If there is a search clue, the next record with a match for the clue will be found.

When (and if) a record has been found, the position of that record in the file is saved (by the line 'c%=POS'), and the 'SCSEE: ' routine is called to prepare and display the record. 'SCSEE:' will return a value depending on the key pressed during inspection of the record. If the key pressed is S or **CLEAR/ON** (which has an ASCII value of 1), then this routine terminates and processing returns to the calling routine. Otherwise, the next record (in the file, or matching the search clue) is made current.

'SCSEE:' – and the utility function it calls, 'SR%:() – will control the backwards and forwards movement through the records based on the keypresses: the SCFR: routine controls the movement to the next record as a result of pressing the **EXE** key.

When the end of the file has been reached, the `WHILE FIND()..ENDWH` loop ends, and a test is made to see if there has been a search clue. If there has (`IF S$<>""`), and also provided that a record has been found (`IF C%`), a message is displayed briefly, indicating that the end of the file has been reached, and that the last matching record is to be re-displayed. The last matching record is then made current, and processing jumps back to the loop again. If a search clue was given but no match was found (i.e C% = 0, and so '`IF C%`' gives a not-true answer), then an appropriate message is displayed and, this time (since there is no point searching the file again), processing jumps back to the start to receive another potential search clue.

If no search clue was given, then the 'EOF:Last record = ' message is displayed briefly, the last record in the file is made current, and a jump is made back to the loop.

Thus, you will be made quite aware of the situation when you reach the end of the file, and can act accordingly.

Incidentally, if when you examine the procedure you wonder about the names given to the labels - 'GC::' and 'RS::' - these stand for 'Get Clue' and 'Repeat Search' respectively. It is very helpful when creating your own procedures to use meaningful (to you) mnemonics.

Inputs

None. But naturally, the file must have been opened.

Returns

The selected record is made current, for further work (such as amending field-data or deleting) if necessary

Non-OPL functions called

The following non-OPL procedures are called directly by this procedure. These, and any procedures that they call must be entered for STOCK to run.

a) *Utilities*
GI$:()
MSG:()

b) *Stock Control specific routines*
SCSEE:

Globals needed

None. (But you can, if you wish, include the declared and assigned Global 'Q$' for a question mark).

Variables used

C% = Check Holds the record number for the most recently found record in a 'clued' search.
T% = Terminate Holds the value returned by 'SCSEE:', to test for a procedure-terminating keypress.
S$ = String Holds the details for a search clue.

Customizing

Provided that this routine is used when a file has been opened, and provided the routines it calls are available in one form or another, it can be used almost as it stands for any of your own file-handling programs. You will have to name the 'called' routines appropriately, of course, since these routines will be different for your own program to those given in this Chapter.

In fact it is because the called routines must be 'program specific' that it is difficult to turn SCFR: into a general purpose routine: you will find a very similar routine in the BANKER program suite, so you can compare the two to see the subtle differences necessary to suit a specific program.

You may wish to abbreviate the (rather lengthy) scrolling messages – indeed, you may consider the message about which keys to press during a search to be superfluous or unnecessarily long. It can be removed from the procedure, or shortened as you wish, but do remember that it is easy to forget which keys you must press when using a program after even a short period of time.

The Listing

```
SCFR:
LOCAL C%,T%,S$(16)
KSTAT 1
GC::
FIRST
S$=GI$:("Enter clue(or EXE to stepthru)",2)
VIEW(1,"USE EXE=findnext,<N>ext,<B>ack,
[above line continued]   <F>irst,<L>ast,<S>earchover")
RS::
WHILE FIND(S$)
  C%=POS
  T%=SCSEE:
  IF (T%=%S) OR (T%=1)
    RETURN
  ELSE
    NEXT
  ENDIF
ENDWH
IF S$<>""
  IF C%
    MSG:("EOF:Last match=")
    POSITION C%
  ELSE
    MSG:("NO MATCH FOUND")
    GOTO GC::
  ENDIF
ELSE
  MSG:("EOF:Last record=")
  LAST
ENDIF
GOTO RS::
```

3.5 Caption a Stock Record
SCSEE:

What it does

This procedure puts meaningful 'captions' to each of the fields of a record when it is to be displayed on the screen. As you are aware, OPL's `DISP(-1,S$)` function simply displays each field on its own line, which can cause confusion as to which field is which where numbers are concerned. By adding suitable captions, the contents of the file will be more readily understood. (See also under 'SR%:' in Chapter 2).

In addition to the fields actually contained on each Stock record, new 'fields' are generated to display the total stock value, the total VAT to be added to the stock, and the VAT on each individual item: these are included to demonstrate how the information contained on each record can be expanded to give other information you may wish to have available 'at a glance'. You will no doubt wish to modify these elements to produce the information that you want.

The captions given to each field by this routine are as follows:

ITEM: The name or reference for the stock item.
QTY: The quantity currently held in stock.
P/E: The price of each individual item.
SVAL: The value of the stock held for this item.
TVAT: The Total VAT to be added to the stock (based simply on cost price + 15%).
IVAT: The VAT to be added to an individual item of stock.
REOL: The re-ordering level.

Space required

The space required for the procedure, as listed, but without leading spaces or 'REMarks' (see Chapter 2.1) and excluding space required by any of the non-OPL routines called is:
Source + object code: 835 bytes
Object code only: 413 bytes

How it works

A large string array is declared, to hold the all of the caption + field information. Variables are also declared to hold the tab-character (necessary to separate each field for display on its own line), and to hold the calculated stock value.

The stock value is calculated, by multiplying the quantity by the price per item, and then the overall string is built up in easy to follow stages. Notice that numerical values must be converted to strings, using OPL's `NUM$()`, `GEN$()` and `FIX$()` functions. (You'll find information about how to use these functions in your handbook). Notice too that the last line of the record doesn't need to have a tab character.

To keep the final display as neat as possible, and to minimise any possible scrolling of each line, the 'captions' are kept to four characters each, followed by a colon.

Once the string is prepared, a call is made to the utility function SR%:(), to actually display the record. This is described in Chapter 2, but to remind you, SR%:() allows you to use cursor keys to move around the record, and it allows you to use the **N**, **B**, **F**, and **L** keys to move around the file. SR%:() will actually make a new record the 'current' record if one of these keys is pressed. Whatever key is pressed during the inspection of the record, the ASCII value of that key is returned to this procedure. A test is made to see whether a 'terminating' key has been pressed – **S** or **CLEAR/ON** (for Stop), or **EXE** (to continue with the search or move to the next record, depending on whether or not a search clue was given). If a terminating key has been pressed, then the ASCII value of the pressed key is returned from this routine to the calling routine SCFR:() for further appropriate action.

If a terminating key has not been pressed, it is assumed that a new record has been made current, and a jump is made back to the beginning of this routine to prepare the new record for display, as before. If a key other than **N**, **B**, **F** or **L** has been pressed, you'll examine the same record again. In other words, only the keys mentioned have any effect. So don't forget them! (Hence the reminder in the SCFR: routine).

Inputs

When preparing a routine to handle your own requirements, the file must be opened, and you must use the same field names here as when you created and opened the file.

Returns

The ASCII value of the S, **CLEAR/ON** or **EXE** key, whichever was pressed.

Non-OPL functions called

File handling utility

SR%:()

Globals needed

None specifically, but the field variables are, in effect 'Global' provided the file has been opened.

Variables used

a) *Field variables*

These hold information about the current record, as follows:
A.I$ = Item A string holding the item name.
A.Q% = Quantity An integer holding the Quantity held in stock.
A.PE = Price-Each A float holding the Price of Each item.
A.ROL% = Re-Order Level An integer holding the minimum permitted stock level.

b) *Local variables*

S$ = String Holds all of the captions, fields, and tab information.
T$ = Tab Holds the 'tab' character, CHR$(9), which forces a new line in the `DISP(1,S$)` function.
SV = Stock Value A floating point variable to hold the calculated Stock Value for the record under inspection.
C% = Check Holds the return value from the SR%:() utility function.

Customizing

Here's where you can really tailor your program to do what you want. As you can see from this routine, in addition to the information that is actually stored for each record, you can calculate other details that you may need to see when the record is displayed. The listing here, for example, calculates the stock value, the amount of VAT to be added to the stock value, and the VAT to be added to each item. These calculations are purely for demonstration. You can make similar calculations to suit your own needs, bearing in mind only that the field information must be available to make the calculations. (You can also, of course, change the order of displayed lines)

To give another example, supposing you wished to know 'up front' (i.e., within the first two lines of the display) if the stock is below the minimum level, and if so, how much it would cost to bring it up to the minimum level + 1. Immediately after the '`S$="ITEM: "+A.I$+T$`' line you would add a test to check the quantity in stock against the re-order level, and if it is low, you would signal the fact, then add in the cost. So the extra lines would look something like this:

```
IF A.Q%<A.ROL%
  S$=S$+"LOW: "
  S$=S$+FIX$(A.PE*((A.ROL%-A.QTY)+1),2,9)
S$=S$+"TO RESTOCK"+T$
ENDIF
```

As you can see, numeric values must be converted to strings before they are 'tacked' onto the end of S$. This example, together with those written into the procedure, should help you to prepare a record display that gives you exactly the information you want from your records.

The Listing

```
SCSEE:
LOCAL S$(250),T$(1),SV,C%
T$=CHR$(9)
AG::
SV=A.Q%*A.PE
S$="ITEM:"+A.I$+T$
S$=S$+"QTY:"+GEN$(A.Q%,7)+T$
S$=S$+"P/E:"+GEN$(A.PE,7)+T$
S$=S$+"SVAL:"+GEN$(SV,7)+T$
S$=S$+"TVAT:"+FIX$(SV*.15,2,9)+T$
S$=S$+"IVAT:"+FIX$(A.PE*.15,2,9)+T$
S$=S$+"REOL:"+NUM$(A.ROL%,7)
C%=SR%:(S$)
IF (C%=13) OR (C%=%S) OR (C%=1)
  RETURN C%
ENDIF
GOTO AG::
```

3.6 Update a Stock Record
SCUD:

What it does

This short routine enables you to amend any field in any record of the opened Stock Control file. In practice, you would select the option to 'Update' from the main menu and then select the record to be changed (via the SCFR: routine described previously). The record having been selected, you are then offered a menu which identifies the fields of the record. You can continue selecting fields to change until you choose to end - either by pressing the **EXE** key, or by selecting 'END' from the menu.

Space required

The space required for the procedure, as listed, but without leading spaces or 'REMarks' (see Chapter 2.1) and excluding space required by any of the non-OPL routines called is:
Source + object code: 517 bytes
Object code only: 269 bytes

How it works

This routine is fairly straightforward. It contains two DO...UNTIL loops, one nested within the other. The first or outer loop allows you to continue selecting records to change, until you choose 'FINISH' from the associated menu. The second or inner loop allows you to continue selecting record fields to edit until you choose 'END' from the inner loop menu. Once the choice of a record and a field has been made, the selected field is re-assigned by a call to the relevant editing utility (described in detail in Chapter 2). These utilities won't allow an incorrect entry – if you enter alphabetic letters while editing a number, you will have to re-edit that number. If you insert a decimal point in an integer field's number, the relevant utility will simply chop out all the decimal places.

When all the changes to a particular record have been made the OPL UPDATE command is used to re-write the record to the file.

It has been mentioned before, but it is important tou understand that what actually happens is the original record is erased, and the new, amended record is written to the end of the file. In other words, changing records also changes their order in the file.

Inputs

The file must be opened with the fields declared as used within the routine.

Returns

None. The selected record or records are updated.

Non-OPL functions called

File handling utilities

ES$:()
EI%:()
EF:()

Globals needed

None specifically, but the field variables are, in effect 'Global' provided the file has been opened.

Variables used

a) *Field variables*

These hold information about the current record, as follows:
A.I$ = Item A string holding the item name.
A.Q% = Quantity An integer holding the Quantity held in stock.
A.PE = Price-Each A float holding the Price of Each item.
A.ROL% = Re-Order Level An integer holding the minimum permitted stock level.

b) *Local variables*

C% = Check Holds the result of the record field selection.

Customizing

This routine can be a 'prototype' for an updating routine in any of your own programs. Whatever field names you use when you create and open the file, those field names must be used here. Equally, you will want the menu options to reflect the content of those fields. You will, of course, need a routine similar to 'SCFR:' in order to select the record to be updated, and you will need to call that routine in place of SCFR:.

The Listing

```
SCUD:
LOCAL C%
DO            :REM Outer record-selecting loop
  SCFR:
  DO          :REM Inner field-selecting loop
    C%=MENU("Item,Stock,Price,Min-level,End")
    IF C%=1
      A.I$=ES$:(A.I$)
    ELSEIF C%=2
      A.Q%=EI%:(A.Q%)
    ELSEIF C%=3
      A.PE=EF:(A.PE,2)
    ELSEIF C%=4
      A.ROL%=EI%:(A.ROL%)
    ELSE C%=0
    ENDIF
  UNTIL C%=0
  UPDATE
UNTIL MENU("ANOTHER,FINISH")<>1
```

3.7 Delete a Stock Record
SCDR:

What it does

This very short routine is called when you wish to delete a record from your opened file. To make sure that you really do want to delete the record, a check is made first. Having confirmed the deletion, the record is duly erased from the file, never to be seen again.

Space required

The space required for the procedure, as listed, but without leading spaces or 'REMarks' (see Chapter 2.1) and excluding space required by any of the non-OPL routines called is:
Source + object code: 150 bytes
Object code only: 85 bytes

How it works

A call is made to the SCFR: Stock control routine, to find the record you wish to erase. When chosen, the record becomes the 'current' record. You are then asked to confirm the deletion: the first six characters of the record's item field are displayed to remind you of the selected record. The confirmation (or otherwise) is obtained by a call to the file-handling utility YORN%:. If the result of this call is a '1' (signifying yes), the record is erased. Otherwise, the record is left in the file and a return made to the main Stock control menu. Note how simple the test for 'Yes' is: it is not necessary to do anything on selection of 'No' except leave this routine.

Inputs

None.

Returns

None.

Non-OPL functions called

a) *File-handling utility*

YORN%:

b) *Specific to the Stock Control program*

SCFR:

Globals needed

Q$ must have been declared and assigned to the question mark character CHR$(63).

Variables used

Field variable

A.I$ = Item Used to identify the item to be deleted.

Customizing

This procedure is easy to adapt to your own programs: You will, of course, have to appropriately name the call to your 'find-a-record' routine (here called SCFR:), and the field used to identify the record.

The Listing

```
SCDR:         :REM This is the name of the routine
SCFR:         :REM This is a 'call' to SCFR:
PRINT"Delete",LEFT$(A.I$,6);Q$
IF YORN%:
  ERASE
ENDIF
```

3.8 Analyse Stock File
SCTV:

What it does

This routine provides the answer two specific questions about the Stock Control file:

What is the total value of the stock held?
Which items are below the re-order level?

This is the routine selected when 'TOTALS' is chosen from the main Stock Control menu. It immediately offers a further menu with the options 'STOCK-VALUE', 'LOW-STOCKS' and 'END', and will return to the main Stock Control Menu when 'END' is selected or the **CLEAR/ON** key is pressed.

The 'STOCK-VALUE' option inspects every record in turn, calculates the total value of the stock item, and adds that total to an 'accumulator'. That total is then displayed. The 'LOW-STOCKS' option inspects each record in turn, and displays the name of those items that have a stock lower than or equal to the re-order level, together with the number of items needed to take the stock level above the re-order level. The information for each low stock is displayed until a key is pressed.

Space required

The space required for the procedure, as listed, but without leading spaces or 'REMarks' (see Chapter 2.1) and excluding space required by any of the non-OPL routines called is:
Source + object code: 563 bytes
Object code only: 259 bytes

How it works

The two analytical routines in this procedure are contained within a `DO...UNTIL` loop, so that both analyses can be undertaken without having to return to the Stock Control menu.

For the 'Total Stock Value' analysis, the variable holding the accumulation of the value (TV) is first 'cleared' by assigning a zero to it. This is necessary to prevent a repeated analysis giving a false answer: any value already in TV will be added in 'next time round'. The file is set to the first record, then for each record in turn (until the end-of-file) the stock value for the item is calculated and added into TV. The total value is then displayed with a suitable message until a key is pressed. (CHR$(237) is a close approximation of the 'pound' sign).

The 'Low Stocks' analysis follows a similar process. The file is set to the first record, then each record is examined in turn to see whether the stock quantity (A.Q%) is less than or equal to the re-order level (A.ROL%). If it is, a suitable message is assembled, naming the item and giving the quantity needed to restore the stock to the minimum permitted level + 1. This is displayed on a scrolling line using OPL's VIEW function, so that it remains on display until a key is pressed.

Inputs

None. But the file must be opened.

Returns

None.

Non-OPL functions called

None.

Globals needed

None.

Variables used

a) *Field variables*

A.I$ = Item The name or reference of the item in the current record.
A.Q% = Quantity The quantity of item in stock for the current record.
A.PE = Price Each The cost of the item for the current record.
A.ROL% = Re-order level The re-order level of the item in the current record.

b) *Local variables*

TV = Total Value Holds the accumulating total value for all the stock items.

C% = Check Holds the result of the menu selection.

Customizing

This routine demonstrates how to obtain analyses of the overall file, and can provide a basis for your own routines. You add the required option name(s) in the menu string, then 'call' appropriate routine(s) written to act on selection of the option(s).

Note that the hyphens between menu words are important to avoid problems when selecting from the menu.

The Listing

```
SCTV:
LOCAL TV,C%
DO
  C%=MENU("STOCK-VALUE,LOW-STOCKS,END")
 IF C%=1
   TV=0
   FIRST
   DO
      TV=TV+(A.Q%*A.PE)
     NEXT
   UNTIL EOF
   PRINT "TOTAL VALUE:"
   PRINTCHR$(237);TV
  GET
  ELSEIF C%=2
  FIRST
 DO
   IF A.Q%<=A.ROL%
     VIEW(1,"A.I$+"low by"+NUM$(A.ROL%+1-A.Q%,5))
   ENDIF
   NEXT
 UNTIL EOF
   ELSE C%=0
   ENDIF
UNTIL C%=0
```

3.9 Printout Stock Records

SCPR:

What it does

This routine provides a formatted print-out of the information that's contained in each record in the Stock file, together with a calculated 'item stock value', all under suitable headings. The total stock value is then printed out. Obviously you will need to have a printer connected to your Organiser, properly set up using Psion's Comms Link. If you don't have a printer, you can ignore this routine (and delete the option from the main Stock control menu, also deleting the 'ELSEIF C%=5' line and re-writing the line 'C%=6' to read 'C%=5', in STOCK:).

Space required

The space required for the procedure, as listed, but without leading spaces or 'REMarks' (see Chapter 2.1) and excluding space required by any of the non-OPL routines called is:
Source + object code: 678 bytes
Object code only: 318 bytes

How it works

A 'tab' character is defined, to help make spacing and positioning of the print-out easier. The first record in the file is made current, then the headings are printed out on one line. Then comes a DO...UNTIL loop, to print out the data from each record until the end-of-the-file.

Prior to the print-out of each record, the item value is calculated, and the resulting sum added into an accumulator (for the total-stock-value print-out at the end). To ensure proper spacing of each record, the FIL$:() utility is called for the item name string, and the FIX$() and NUM$() functions are used in their 'right-justifying' form. Notice the use of semi-colons in the LPRINT statements to keep the printout of each record on one line.

Inputs

None. But the file must be open.

Returns

None.

Non-OPL functions called

FIL$:()

Globals needed

None.

Variables used

a) *Field variables*

A.I$ = Item The name or reference of the item in the current record.
A.Q% = Quantity The quantity of item in stock for the current record.
A.PE = Price Each The cost of the item for the current record.
A.ROL% = Re-order level The re-order level of the item in the current record.

b) *Local variables*

T$ = Tab The 'tab' character for aligning the print-out display.
IV = Item Value Holds the total value of the stock for the current record.
TV = Total Value Holds the running total of all the total item values.

Customizing

This procedure has been prepared to show you 'how it is done'. If you have a printer, it is probably best to enter the routine as it is here so that you can see the print-out obtained, before adjusting it to suit your own requirements.

When writing a similar routine for your own program(s), the main point to note is that you must (obviously) use the same field names that you used when the file was created and opened. Getting the figures to line up nicely can take a little 'juggling' – adjusting the tabs and the justifying factors in the number-to-string conversions. You could choose to ignore these conversions – but the print-out will then look quite a mess and be difficult to read, with nothing lining up at all. Also, by using the FIX$() function, you can ensure that calculations do not result in more than two decimal places being printed out.

You can, of course, add your own analytical requirements to the print-out, not just for each record (within the DO...UNTIL EOF loop), but also for the file as a whole at the end. If you know the codes your printer needs for 'bold' characters and so on, you could enter these too as characters (CHR$(*ASCII*)), or by building up a string.

The Listing

```
SCPR:
LOCAL T$(1),TV,IV
T$=CHR$(9)           :REM 'Tab' character
FIRST
LPRINT"ITEM";T$;T$;
LPRINT"QTY";T$;T$;
LPRINT"RE-OL";T$;T$;
LPRINT " I/COST";T$;T$;
LPRINT"I/VALUE"
LPRINT
DO
  IV=A.Q%*A.PE
  TV=TV+IV
  LPRINT FIL$:(A.I$,7);T$;T$;
  LPRINT NUM$(A.Q%,-5);T$;T$;
  LPRINT NUM$(A.ROL%,-5);T$;T$;
  LPRINT FIX$(A.PE,2,-9);T$;T$;
  LPRINT FIX$(IV,2,-9)    :REM no semi-colon here
  NEXT
UNTIL EOF
LPRINT
LPRINT"TOTAL STOCK VALUE (Ex VAT)";
LPRINT CHR$(23);FIX$(TV,2,9)
```

CHAPTER 4

Bank Account Handler Program

4.1 Keeping Your Balance

...without losing your head

This program has been developed specifically to demonstrate how two (or more) files can be handled at the same time on Organiser, and, perhaps more pertinently, to look after your personal finances. The basic requirements for the program are essentially the same as those given in Chapters 1 and 3 – we need to be able create and open files, to add records and so on. Before we go any further, let us have a look at what a typical 'Bank Account' handling program should do – the 'specification'.

The purpose of the program is to keep track of all expenditures and income. To do this, we will need perform the following operations.

1. Record every transaction. This involves being able to:
   a) debit the account for payments made by cheque.
   b) debit the account for withdrawals from 'Autobanks' or 'Cash tills'.
   c) debit the account for Standing Orders – *automatically*.
   d) credit the account.

For all of these, the transaction record should contain the following details:
   i) An identifying reference (Cheque number, AUTo-bank etc.)
   ii) The amount paid out or paid in.
   iii) Brief details of the transaction.
   iv) The date of the transaction.

2. For Standing Orders, it must be possible to
   a) add new Standing Orders or delete paid-up Standing Orders.
   b) amend the amounts paid – or the period of payments (consider your mortgage, for example).

For these, the Standing Order records need to contain details about:
   i) Who the payment is to (for identification)
   ii) The amount to be paid
   iii) The total number of monthly payments due.

3. For Bank Statement verification, it is necessary to know which debits and credits have not yet reached the bank, so that an adjustment can be made to the figure on the Statement for comparison purposes.

4. It must be possible to examine or browse through the transaction records, and ideally to observe the state of the bank balance after each transaction. It must be possible to examine the 'Standing Orders', to see how many payments are still to be made, for example. If you have a printer, you would also want to be able to print out the transaction and Standing Order records.

Quite a specification. The program given in this Chapter demonstrates just one way to meet all of these requirements.

Where does the money go?

It is probably obvious that at least two files are needed: one to hold the transaction records, and one to hold details of the Standing Orders. Now, what about the current bank balance. Where should we store this value?

Three options are available. We can:

a) Store the current balance in a third file.
b) Store a 'current' balance with each transaction record.
c) Calculate the current balance when it is needed.

Let us examine each of these options in turn. Storing the current balance in a third file (option (a)) would mean that you couldn't examine an individual record to see what the balance was 'at that time'. It would also mean that, when verifying statements, it would be difficult to locate the point where things go wrong (if they do) as a result of an incorrect entry: only the final figure could be checked against the bank statement.

Storing the current balance along with each transaction (option (b)) has the advantage that the 'state of affairs' can be examined from one transaction to the next. There is, however, a disadvantage: if any of the details in a transaction record are changed, it will affect the order of all the records following it – Organiser changes the order of records when they're updated remember. If the cash details are changed, it will be difficult to 'run' the change of *balance* through the records, without using up a considerable amount of memory space.

The fact that Organiser changes the order of records that have been updated creates problems for the third option (c) too – especially if one wants to check the balance after each record. Ensuring that the records are examined or operated on in a set sequence irrespective of their actual order in Organiser would entail having a 'sequencing' field for each record, so each record has a fixed record number. If a record is deleted, it would be a simple matter to re-number all those that follow it: the record number would, of course, need to be hidden from view so that it couldn't be edited. However, if one is going to add a field to each record, one may as well use that field to hold the actual bank balance resulting from the associated transaction – and not waste time (and space) with all the sorting and ancillary routines that would be required.

The BANKER program consequently uses option (b) – storing the current balance in the associated transaction record. It means that, once entered, a transaction record must not be changed or deleted. This shouldn't present a problem: you can't alter cheques and so on once they have been paid, and it is an easy matter to correct a wrong monetary entry, by entering a 'dummy' transaction. Thus there is no provision in the BANKER program to amend a transaction record – and to maintain program accuracy, you shouldn't add a transaction-amending routine without a host of other routines to maintain the records in their correct order!

Entering the program

The BANKER program has been written as a dozen or so short(ish) routines, so that, when running, it doesn't occupy too much space at a time. Organiser loads procedures from where they are saved into its RAM area for 'running' only as they are 'called'.

With BANKER, there will rarely be more than three procedures in RAM at a time. The alternative of having fewer but longer routines would mean considerably more 'running space' is required – leaving less space for your files (and Diary).

Practically all of the routines are dependent on files being opened, and on other procedures being present in Organiser. This makes it almost impossible (as with the Stock Control program) to provide sensible 'Test Programs' to check each procedure as it is entered.

A recommended approach would be to first enter the main BANKER procedure along with 'BRD:', 'BNSO:' and 'BUSO:' (together with the file-handling utilities they require from Chapter 2), and to test the 'create or open a file' options by creating for yourself a 'dummy' file. Then as you add all the routines necessary to perform a specific option, that option can be tested to ensure that there are no errors. Once you have proved the program and perhaps tailored it to your own needs, you can erase the 'dummy' file.

Space required

Assuming all the routines are entered as listed, but without leading spaces or REMarks (see Chapter 2.1), the amount of space needed to save the BANKER program – and all of the utility routines called by BANKER – is as follows (give or take a byte or two).

Utility routines called by BANKER:
Source + object code: 2812 bytes
Object code only: 1263 bytes

BANKER *specific routines*:
Source + object code: 6600 bytes
Object code only: 3218 bytes

Combined space required:
Source + object code: 9412 bytes
Object code only: 4481 bytes

Note that once the utility routines have been entered, they can be used for *any* file handling program as 'extra' OPL words. Thus, the amount of space required for both of the STOCK CONTROL and BANKER programs (say), would be the total space required for all of the program-specific routines, plus the space required for the utilities called: both programs use the same utility routines, remember.

4.2 Using the Banker Program

Setting up a file

BANKER is a fairly comprehensive program suite, and while the 'instructions for its use' will become apparent as and when you enter each of the individual procedures (and when you run it), it can be useful to have an idea of how it operates before you start.

When you run BANKER, the screen will clear and you will be asked to enter the file name for your transactions. If you have already created a file, you simply enter its name (if you forget to enter the location where the file has been saved, you will be prompted for it).

If you haven't created a file, or you wish to create another file (for another year, perhaps), or if Organiser can't find the file name you entered, you will be asked if you wish to create a new file with the name you entered. Choose 'no', and the program terminates. Choose 'yes', and the necessary files are created (yes, *files*: but as far as you are concerned, they are referenced by the name you entered).

When creating a new file, you will be asked for the Current Bank Balance. This will be the opening balance for all of your transactions to follow. This balance must include *all* credits and debits that may not have reached the bank yet: in other words, the amount you consider the balance to be, not what is on the Bank Statement. An 'opening balance' record will be created, with the current date automatically included.

You will then be asked if there are any Standing Orders. Answering 'yes' will take you through a series of questions about the Standing Orders: for each one you will be asked to enter the recipient, the amount, the number of monthly payments – and whether a payment is due in the current month. This last question is important because the program will automatically update all Standing Orders on the *first day* of the month. So if a payment is due in the current month, it will be missed if the file is created on, say, the second day of the month.

Note that the program presented here does not cater for quarterly or annual standing orders.

When you see the main menu...

If you are using the program for the first time in a month – or perhaps after a number of months, all the Standing Order payments will be made automatically (for every month from the month of the last payment to the current month). A 'transaction' record will be created with a reference 'S/O'. The total payments made will be entered as the 'transaction', along with details "S/Orders to ..." followed by the name of the current month. The date that payments were actually made (by the Organiser) is also recorded.

The Standing Order file record will also be updated automatically: the 'number of payments due' is reduced by one for each month payments have been made (so you will always be able to see how many payments are left), and the *month* of the payment is recorded (this information is needed by the Organiser so it can tell whether payments are due).

You will then be presented with a 'menu' of options:

```
SEE TRANSACT
CHANGE-SO VERIFY
PRINTOUT END
```

The function of these options is described in the following paragraphs.

The SEE option

Selecting SEE takes you to a further menu

```
RECORDS S/ORDERS
```

from which you can choose to look at your transaction records or Standing Orders. You can then browse back and forth through the chosen file, examining each record, or you can find specific entries based on a search clue. During this process, the keys are pre-defined as follows

N takes you to the next record in the file. If you're already at the last record, it will be re-displayed.

L takes you back to the previous record in the file. If you are at the first record, it will be re-displayed.

F takes you straight to the first record in the file (with the Standing Order file, this won't necessarily be the first you entered – if you have made amendments).

L takes you to the last record in the file.

S or **CLEAR/ON** will terminate the examination of the file.

EXE will take you to the next record in the file (like **N**) if a search clue was not given: if a search clue was given, it will take you to the next record that has a match for the clue. If no more records match the clue, the last matching record will be re-displayed. If no records matching the clue are found, you will be able to enter another search clue or simply dive straight in and browse.

The TRANSACT option

This will be your choice when you wish to make a Debit or Credit entry. You make your selection from a further menu:

```
DEBIT CREDIT END
```

You will then be prompted to enter information, as follows:

Reference: This is your reference for the transaction. The suggestion is you enter meaningful 'codes' – the last three digits of a cheque for withdrawals, 'AUT' for a cash-till payment, 'SAL' for when you pay in your salary, and so on. If at this point you choose not to make an entry after all, pressing **EXE** will return you to the 'DEBIT, CREDIT, END' menu, from which you can return to the main BANKER menu.

Amount to Credit (or **Debit**) The display will indicate 'Credit' or 'Debit' according to your initial choice: if you have made a mistake in your choice, simply press **EXE** and you will be returned to the 'DEBIT, CREDIT, END' menu. Otherwise, you simply enter the amount involved as a decimal number.

Brief Details This is where you enter a short reminder of what the transaction is all about – 'NEW DATAPAK', 'GAS BILL', 'SOLD CAR', for example.

Once these are entered, the current date and the resulting balance are both entered into the record *automatically* by the program, and the record is appended to the transaction file. You are then returned to the 'DEBIT, CREDIT, END' menu so that you can make another transaction, or finish by selecting 'END' or pressing the **CLEAR/ON** key.

The CHANGE-SO option

This takes you to another menu:

```
ADD CHANGE
DELETE END
```

These options allow you to manipulate the records in the *Standing Order* file, as follows.

ADD takes you through the process described earlier for creating a Standing Order entry. You will be asked the name of the recipient, the sum due per month, the number of monthly payments to be made, and whether payment is due in the current month. The record is then added to the Standing Order file.

CHANGE allows you to give a search clue or browse through the Standing Order records, to select the one that needs changing. (The process is as described under the heading 'SEE', on page 123). Once the record has been chosen, another menu appears:

```
NAME AMOUNT
MONTHS-LEFT END
```

From this menu you can choose at will to make changes to the various fields of the record. When you have finished, select 'END' or press the **CLEAR/ON** key to return to the main BANKER menu.

DELETE is similar to 'CHANGE': you give a search clue or browse through the Standing Order files to select the record to delete. You will then be asked to confirm the deletion, and if you confirm, it will be deleted.

The VERIFY option

This option helps you to compare the bottom line on your Bank Statement with the balance in the last record of your transaction file. To do this, the procedure is as follows:

a) First select 'SEE' from the main BANKER menu, and go through your transaction file, record by record, ticking off each transaction on the Bank Statement. Make a list of all the debits and a list of all the credits that don't appear on the Bank statement as you go.
b) When this has been done, select the VERIFY option from the main BANKER menu. You will be asked to enter all the DEBITS (the cash sums only) from your list, one by one – entering a '0' to finish. You will then be asked to enter all the CREDITS on your list, ending again by entering a '0'. Thus you will have entered all the amounts for the transactions that do *not* appear on the Bank statement.
c) You will then be asked to enter the Bank balance at the bottom of your Bank Statement.

The program will then make the necessary adjustments and compare the figures saved in your file with the Bank statement figures, and report the result with a suitable message – hopefully "Records show BALANCE with Bank statement". If there is an error, you will be told the amount of difference, and whether your figures are greater than or less than those on the Bank statement.

The PRINTOUT option

This option is for those with a printer. It first prints out a table of all the Standing Order information, under the headings NAME, AMOUNT, NOP (number of payments left), and LAST PAID. It then prints out a table of transaction records, under headings DATE, REF, AMOUNT, DETAILS and BALANCE.

A final word

As you will appreciate, BANKER is quite an extensive program – with a reasonable amount of flexibility for customizing. Each of the procedures that go to make up the program is described in detail, so that its operation can be understood and emulated in programs of your own. At the same time, it provides a useful facility that makes looking after the Bank account straightforward.

4.3 The Main Banker Routine

BANKER:

What it does

This is the main controlling routine for the BANKER program. It incorporates the routines to 'create' and 'open' a file, and once a file has been opened, it checks to see whether it is time to deduct Standing Order payments. It then allows repeated choice from a menu of options, until 'END' is selected from the menu, or the **CLEAR/ON** key is pressed.

Details of how to use the BANKER program are given in Chapter 4.2.

Space required

The space required for the procedure, as listed, but without leading spaces or 'REMarks' (see Chapter 2.1) and excluding space required by any of the non-OPL routines called is:

Source + object code: 1364 bytes
Object code only: 658 bytes

How it works

If you compare this routine with the main controlling routine for the Stock Control program (Chapter 3.2), you will notice they both follow a basic format: the same format can be used for your own file-handling programs. For the BANKER program, however, we need two files to be created and opened, one to hold the transaction records, and one to hold the Standing Order records.

To save you from having to enter both of the file names, (which must obviously be different), the name entered when asked for the 'Bank Filename' is used to generate the name for the associated Standing Order file. The last two characters of the entered file name are replaced by the letters 'SO'. This operation is performed whether the files exist or not: if they don't exist, you are asked if you wish to create a new file. If 'yes', both files are created, with the transaction file as logical file 'A', and the Standing Order file as logical file 'B'.

These logical file letters are used to identify the files throughout the rest of the program.

When creating the files, it is necessary to set up the 'starting points'. For the transaction file, this means entering the 'Current Bank Balance'. The first record is then created as the 'Opening Balance', tagged with the reference 'CR' (for a 'credit') and the current date (through the BRD: procedure), derived from Organiser's built in system. The program then asks for the Standing Order details, each of which is added to the Standing Order file as a separate record. The Standing Orders are entered by a call to the 'BNSO:' procedure.

If the files already exist, they are opened in the same way as when they were created. Note that a check is made to see that both files exist: if for some reason only one of the files is present in Organiser, an attempt will be made to create both files and, since one already exists, an error will occur. This has not been error-trapped. In fact the only error-trapping undertaken in the 'create or open' routines is that provided by the utility GFN$:. It is assumed that you will enter a correct file name using only the permitted characters (see your Handbook).

Once the create or open routine has been completed, a call is made to the 'BUSO:' procedure, which checks through each of the Standing Orders in turn to see whether any should be 'paid' (you may have added a new one the last time you used the program). You'll find further details about this routine in Chapter 4.6.

The BANKER routine then enters a DO...UNTIL loop, allowing you to choose from a menu of options until either 'END' is selected or the **CLEAR/ON** key is pressed. Both files are then closed. (Technically, this isn't necessary, since all files are automatically closed when a program terminates. But it is a good habit to get into).

Non-OPL functions called

All of these functions and routines must be entered.

a) *File Handling utilities*

GFN$:()
GI$:()
YORN%:

b) *Banker specific routines*

BRD:
BNSO:
BUSO:
BSEE:
BUPD:
BASO:
BCBS:
BPRO:

Globals needed

None.

Variables used

a) *Global*

These are available to the entire program

Q$ = Question Used to hold the question mark character.
F$ = Filename Holds the main transaction file name.
B$ = Bank file Used to hold the program-generated name for the Standing Orders file.

b) *Local variables*

C% = Check Used to hold the selected menu option.

c) *Transaction file record field-names*

Note: These will all be prefixed by 'A.' when used as variables by the various routines in the BANKER program

R$ = Reference Holds the reference for a transaction – the cheque number, or a suitable code.
D$ = Details Holds brief details about the transaction.
S = Sum Holds the amount of the transaction – either a credit or a debit.
B = Balance Holds the latest balance, taking into account the current transaction.
DY% = Day Holds the day-of-the-month information.
MN% = Month Holds the month number.
YR% = Year Holds the year.

d) *Standing Order file record field-names*

Note: These will all be prefixed with 'B.' when used by the various routines of the BANKER program.

I$ = Identity Holds the name of the recipient for the Standing Order.
A = Amount Holds the monthly sum due for the Standing Order.
NOP% = Number Of Payments Holds the number of monthly payments due on the Standing Order.
PM% = Paid month Holds as a number the month that the last payment was made.

Customizing

Any routines that you wish to add to the program – for analytical purposes, perhaps – should be 'called' in the final loop. As an example, you may wish to have a routine that searches through all of the transaction records, totalling the amounts paid for electricity and fuel. You could add a series of such routines, selected from their own menu. The routine holding that menu – and providing the 'calls to the analytical routines, could be called 'BANA:' (Banker Analysis). You could then add 'ANALYSIS' to the BANKER menu, between PRINTOUT and END say, with the call 'ELSEIF C%=6 :BANA:'.

You may wish to be given the current bank balance before being presented with the main menu of options. To do this, simply add a few lines immediately before the menu DO loop - making the last record of the 'A' file current, and displaying the balance (field 'A.B'). Thus, you could have something like:

```
USE A
LAST
PRINT"CURRENT BALANCE"
PRINT A.B
GET
```

You will appreciate that everyone has their own ideas regarding the information they wish to obtain from a file of records, and it would be impossible for any book to satisfy them all. The 'BANKER' program gives you the basis on which to work, not just for further development of this program, but for the creation of a similar program to meet your own needs. It could be adapted, for example, to handle the accounts of a small business. Similarly the techniques used for handling two files can be used to develop other types of program altogether – a small pay-roll, perhaps, where employee details are held in one file, and tax details in another.

The Listing *(continues overleaf)*

```
BANKER:
GLOBAL Q$(1),F$(10),B$(10)
LOCAL C%
Q$=CHR$(63)
F$=GFN$:("Bank Filename"+Q$)
B$=LEFT$(F$,8)+"SO"
IF EXIST (F$) AND EXIST (B$)
  OPEN F$,A,R$,D$,S,B,DY%,MN%,YR%
  OPEN B$,B,I$,A,NOP%,PM%
 ELSE
  CLS
  PRINT"Create New File"
  IF YORN%:=0
    STOP
  ELSE
    CREATE F$,A,R$,D$,S,B,DY%,MN%,YR%
    A.B=VAL(GI$:("Current Bank Balance",0))
    A.D$="Opening Balance"
    A.R$="CR"
    BRD:
    APPEND
    CREATE B$,B,I$,A,NOP%,PM%
    CLS
    PRINT"Any S/Orders";Q$
    IF YORN%:
      BNSO:
    ELSE          :REM These lines
      B.PM%=0     :REM are for the
      APPEND      :REM earlier models
      ERASE       :REM of Organiser
    ENDIF
  ENDIF
ENDIF
BUSO:
DO
```

```
  C%=MENU("SEE,TRANSACT,CHANGE-S/O,VERIFY,
[line continued]      PRINTOUT,END")
  IF C%=1
    BSEE:
  ELSEIF C%=2
    BUPD:
  ELSEIF C%=3
    BASO:
  ELSEIF C%=4
    BCBS:
  ELSEIF C%=5
    PRINT"Press key when  Printer ready"
    GET
    BPRO:
  ELSE C%=0
  ENDIF
UNTIL C%=0
CLOSE
CLOSE
```

4.4 Add Date to a Banker Record

BRD:

What it does

In three different places in the Banker program, the current date needs to be added to a record being created for the transaction file. It makes sense, therefore, to perform the operation as a short procedure. This is it.

Space required

The space required for the procedure as listed, is:
Source + object code: 106 bytes
Object code only: 62 bytes

How it works

The transaction file is made current, and the appropriate fields are assigned from Organiser's built in date functions. The full record is added to the file by the calling routine.

Inputs

None.

Returns

The appropriate record fields assigned with the current date.

Non-OPL functions called

None.

Globals needed

None.

Variables used

Transaction file field-names

A.DY% = Day Holds the day-of-the-month information.
A.MN% = Month Holds the month number.
A.YR% = Year Holds the year.

The Listing

```
BRD:
USE A
A.DY%=DAY
A.MN%=MONTH
A.YR%=YEAR
```

4.5 Add a Standing Order

BNSO:

What it does

This is a typical routine for adding a new record to a file: specifically, it adds details of a new Standing Order to the Standing Order file for the BANKER program. It allows an immediate return to the calling routine should the first entry – the recipient for the Standing Order – be blank (as a result of pressing the **EXE** key). The routine continues to 'loop' until the user selects 'END' or presses the **CLEAR/ON** key after entering all the details for one Standing Order record, thus enabling a number of Standing Orders to be entered without having to return to the main menu.

Space required

The space required for the procedure, as listed, but without leading spaces or 'REMarks' (see Chapter 2.1) and excluding space required by any of the non-OPL routines called is:
Source + object code: 644 bytes
Object code only: 309 bytes

How it works

The Standing Order file, opened as the logical 'B' file by the main Banker routine, is made current. The record-entering loop uses the `GI$:()` utility to display suitable messages and to obtain the required inputs for each of the fields of the record.

A test is made to check whether there has been an input for the first field: if no input has been made, a return is made to the calling routine. This allows the user to correct an inadvertent selection of the routine either from the main Banker menu or by choosing 'ANOTHER' after one record has been completed.

For the Standing Orders to be made 'automatically' the first time Banker is used in any given month, one of the fields holds the last month that a payment has been made. When creating the record, if no payment is required during the current month, then the 'last month of payment' is the current month, derived from Organiser's MONTH command. If payment is required during the current month, then this field is set to the previous month. The next time the program is run, the payment will then be made.

Returns

The routine adds a record or records to the Standing Order file.

Non-OPL functions called

GI$:()

Globals needed

Q$ This will have been declared and assigned the question mark character (CHR$(63)) by the main Banker program.

Variables used

a) *Field variables*

B.I$ = Item The name of the recipient for the Standing Order.
B.A = Amount The monthly sum to be paid out.
B.NOP% = Number of Payments The number of monthly payments that have to be made.
B.PM% = Paid to Month The Month that the 'last payment' was made. When creating the record, this will either be the current month or the 'previous month' – to indicate that a payment is due.

b) *Local variable*

C% = Check Holds the response to the question - 'Payment this month?'.

Customizing

The messages to be displayed on the screen are deliberately quite explicit and long. You may feel that they are unnecessarily long, and that you will be able to follow shorter messages. Cutting a message down by 10 bytes will actually save 30 bytes in the Organiser when the program is run – 10 in the source file, 10 in the object file, and 10 when the object file is reloaded into RAM for running. So it is well worth pruning messages – but not to the point where, when using the program, you can't work out what you're supposed to be entering!

The Listing

```
BNSO:
LOCAL C%
USE B
DO
 B.I$=GI$:("Payment to"+Q$,2)
 IF B.I$=""
   RETURN
 ENDIF
 B.A=VAL(GI$:("Monthly Amount",0))
 B.NOP%=VAL(GI$:("Number of MONTHLY payments",1))
 KSTAT 1
 TM::
 C%=VIEW(2,"Is a payment to be made THIS
[line continued]    month (Y or N)")
 IF C%=%Y
   B.PM%=MONTH-1
 ELSEIF C%=%N
   B.PM%=MONTH
 ELSE GOTO TM::
 ENDIF
 APPEND
UNTIL MENU("ANOTHER,END")<>1
```

4.6 Pay Standing Orders
BUSO:

What it does

This is the routine that creates a transaction record, when appropriate, to show the deduction of Standing Order payments. The routine is called at the start whenever the BANKER program is run – since new Standing Orders may have been added during the current or previous month. It also checks to see whether more than one month's payments are due: you may not have run the program for several months. The Standing Order records are also updated by the routine.

Space required

The space required for the procedure, as listed, but without leading spaces or 'REMarks' (see Chapter 2.1) is:
Source + object code: 528 bytes
Object code only: 251 bytes

How it works

This routine demonstrates how Organiser's built in date (or time) functions can be used to automatically update records. The routine first makes the Stock Control file current (opened as logical file 'B'), and then selects the first record of the file.

Then, each record in the Standing Order file is examined in turn. First of all, the Number-of-Payments field is examined: if it is zero, then no more Standing Order payments are needed (hooray!), and there's no more to be done for that record. The next record is selected for examination.

If there are still payments to be made, then the 'Month Last-Paid' field, B.PM%, is compared with the current month in Organiser's built-in calendar. If it isn't the same – meaning that a payment is due – then 'one' is added to the 'Month-Last-Paid' field, the amount to be paid (derived from the 'B.A' field) is added to an accumulating total, and 'one' is deducted from the 'Number-of-Payments'. Note the technique used for adding one to the Month-Last-Paid field. This complex-looking line simply adds one to the current number as long as it is less than 13. When it is equal to 12, then one is added, and the second part of the line immediately deducts 12 – bringing the month number back to one. The month numbers are thus cycled through the numbers 1 to 12.

The Standing Order record is then updated – and the record pointer is set back to the *first* record again! This is something you must watch when writing similar routines: updating a record means 'erasing' it and re-writing a new record at the end of the file. So the record we have been working on is no longer first: it is now last. What was the second record has now become the first record. Hence the reason for re-setting the pointer to 'FIRST'.

The process then continues with the next record. If payments haven't been made for several months, then the entire loop is repeated for each month, until all of the 'Month-Last-Paid' fields show the current month. When this happens, the second test '`IF B.PM%<>MONTH`' fails, so the `NEXT` record is selected, until the End-Of-File is reached.

Once all of the Stock Control records have been brought up-to-date, the variable 'TP' will either be holding the total sum due to make all of the necessary payments, or it will be zero – because no payments are due. If it is not zero, the transaction file is made current, and the last record in that file is made current. That's because the latest balance is held in the last record (we have arranged, remember, that there will be no updating of the transaction records, so they will remain in the order they were entered).

A new record is then automatically created: the reference is 'S/O', and the transaction sum, a Debit, is the accumulated value held in TP. So that you know what has happened when you examine the records, the details are added: 'S/Orders to ...', with the three letter name of the month derived from Organiser's `MONTH` function and the utility `MN$:()` developed in Chapter 2. The bank balance is evaluated and entered into the 'latest bank balance' field, and to complete the transaction record, a call is made to `BRD:` to add the current date. The transaction record is then appended to the file.

As far as you are concerned when running the BANKER program, there will be a momentary pause between selecting the file name and seeing the main Banker menu - even if there are six months payments to catch up on!

Inputs

Both files must have been opened – this is achieved by the main Banker program.

Returns

The Standing Order file and the transaction file are updated if there are any Standing Order payments to be made when switching on.

Non-OPL functions called

MN$:()

Globals needed

None.

Variables used

a) *Standing Order file fields*

B.NOP% = Number of Payments The number of monthly payments left to be made.

B.PM% = Paid Month The last month, as a number, in which Standing Order payments were made for the record.

b) *Transaction file fields*

A.R$ = Reference The code to identify the transaction.

A.S = Sum The amount involved in the transaction.

A.D$ = Details A brief note about the transaction.

A.B = Balance The bank balance after the transaction has been made.

c) *Local variables*

TP = Total payment The variable holding the accumulation of all the Standing Order payments to be made.

Customizing

You may wish to change the messages entered into the fields of the transaction file. When using similar routines in your own programs, do be careful about the way Organiser handles updated records: the results can be very confusing if the right record isn't made current!.

The Listing

```
BUSO:
LOCAL TP
USE B
FIRST
DO
  IF B.NOP%<>0
    IF B.PM%<>MONTH
      B.PM%=B.PM%-1*(B.PM%<13)+12*(B.PM%>=12)
      TP=TP+B.A
      B.NOP%=B.NOP%-1
      UPDATE
      FIRST
    ELSE NEXT
    ENDIF
  ELSE NEXT
  ENDIF
UNTIL EOF
IF TP
  USE A
  LAST
  A.R$="S/O"
  A.S=TP
  A.D$="S/Orders to "+MN$:(MONTH)
  A.B=A.B-A.S
  BRD:
  APPEND
ENDIF
```

4.7 Locate a Record
BLAR:()

What it does

We now come to the routine which locates a record: it follows the format and concept of the Stock Control procedure 'SCFR:' given in Chapter 3.4. This time, however, there are two files involved - the Standing Order file and the transaction file. One could write two procedures, one for each file, along the lines of 'SCFR:'. But this would mean an unnecessary duplication of much of the coding.

With BLAR:(), the choice of file to be examined is determined by an input argument, set by the calling routine. If this argument is a '1' (i.e. 'BLAR:(1)'), the transaction file will be used. If '2', then the Standing Order file will be used.

As with 'SCFR:', two methods are made available for locating a specific record – the 'FIND' technique where a search clue is entered, and the step-through technique. The routine works in conjunction with three other procedures – 'BREC:', 'BSSO:' and the utility SR%:, in the same way that 'SCFR:' works in conjunction with 'SCSEE:' and SR%:.

If no search clue is given, then pressing **EXE** steps through the file record by record. Keys have also been assigned to enable you to step backwards and forwards, as follows:

Pressing...
- **N** will display the next record. If the end of the file is reached, the last record in the file will be re-displayed.
- **B** will display the previous record.
- **F** will display the first record in the file.
- **L** will display the last record in the file.

If a search clue is given – which can relate to any field in the records of the chosen file – then repeatedly pressing **EXE** will search for the next matching record, until the end of the file. The last matching record is then displayed. If there is no matching record, a suitable message is displayed. The keys assigned as detailed above can also be used if a search clue is given, to select other records: however, matching records are found only when the **EXE** key is pressed.

The 'BLAR:()' procedure is used to simply view the filės, and it is also used when you wish to make a change to a record in the Standing Order file, to locate the record that requires changing. To terminate the routine – when the required record has been found, perhaps – press the **S** key or **CLEAR/ON**.

Space required

The space required for the procedure, as listed, but without leading spaces or 'REMarks' (see Chapter 2.1) and excluding space required by any of the non-OPL routines called is:
Source + object code: 811 bytes
Object code only: 363 bytes

How it works

In essence, this routine works in exactly the same way as 'SCFR:' detailed in Chapter 3.4. The input parameter (F%) is used to determine which of the two files is to be searched. If F% = 1, then the transaction file is made current, while if F% = 2, the Standing Order file is made current. A similar test is made for the call to the associated 'record-captioning' routines - 'BREC:' and 'BSSO'. Both of these routines will return the ASCII value of a terminating key press - S or **CLEAR/ON** - or the ASCII value of the **EXE** key. The terminating key presses end the routine, while **EXE** causes the next record or the next matching record to be made current (depending on whether or not a search clue was given).

The end-of-file messages and resulting displays are the same as detailed for SCFR:.

Inputs

The input argument must be
1 for the transaction file
2 for the Standing Order file.

The appropriate input is set by the calling routine, of course.

Returns

The last viewed record in the selected file is made current, for further action if necessary.

Non-OPL functions called

a) *Utility routines*

GI$:()

MSG:()

b) *Banker specific routines*

BREC:

BSSO:

Globals needed

None

Variables used

C% = Check Holds the record number for the most recently found record in a 'clued' search.

T% = Terminate Holds the returned value of the called routine BREC: or BSSO:, to test whether the procedure should be terminated.

S$ = String Holds the search clue information.

Customizing

A similar technique to that used in this routine can be used to view the records in up to four files. For example, if you are also using the Stock Control program, you could dispense with 'SCFR:' by using this routine. To do this you would:

a) Create and Open the Stock Control file as logical file 'C'. This would have to be adjusted throughout the entire Stock Control program – instead of field names beginning 'A.xxx', they would begin 'C.xxx'.

b) Wherever 'SCFR:' is called in the Stock Control program, call 'BLAR:(3)' instead. 'SCFR:' could then be deleted from Organiser.

c) Include an additional test – 'ELSEIF F%=3 :USE C' – at the beginning of BLAR:(), to select the Stock Control file.

d) Include an additional test in the WHILE...ENDWH loop of BLAR:(), to call 'SCSEE:' (Thus: ELSEIF F%=3 :T%=SCSEE:).

Thus, only a few lines extra would be needed to eliminate SCFR:. However, if you do make the change, be sure you correctly identify the Stock Control file as logical file C throughout the Stock Control program. When developing your own file-handling programs using the technique described here, remember that although Organiser can have more than 100 files saved at each location, no more than four can be opened at a time, and only one of those four will be current.

The Listing

```
BLAR:(F%)
LOCAL C%,S$(16),T%
IF F%=1
  USE A
ELSE
  USE B
ENDIF
ST::
FIRST
S$=GI$:("Enter Search clue (or EXE to
(line continued)    stepthru)",2)
VIEW(1,"USE EXE or <N>ext,<B>ack,<F>irst,
(line continued)    <L>ast,<S>earchover")
RS::
WHILE FIND(S$)
  C%=POS
    IF F%=1
      T%=BREC:
    ELSE
      T%=BSSO:
    ENDIF
   IF (T%=%S) OR (T%=1)
      RETURN
    ELSE
      NEXT
    ENDIF
ENDWH
IF S$<>""
  IF C%
    MSG:("EOF:Last match=")
    POSITION C%
  ELSE
    MSG:("NO MATCH FOUND")
    GOTO ST::
  ENDIF
ELSE
  MSG:("EOF:Last record=")
  LAST
ENDIF
GOTO RS::
```

4.8 View Banker Records

BSEE:

What it does

This short routine offers a further menu when 'SEE' is selected from the main BANKER menu, to ascertain whether the transaction file or the Standing Order file is to be viewed.

Space required

The space required for the procedure, as listed, but without leading spaces or 'REMarks' (see Chapter 2.1) and excluding space required by any of the non-OPL routines called is:
Source + object code: 155 bytes
Object code only: 81 bytes

How it works

After displaying the menu, a check is made to see whether the **CLEAR/ON** key has been pressed. If it has, a return is made back to the calling routine. Otherwise the call is made to BLAR:(), with the selected option as the argument.

Inputs

None

Returns

Passes on the selected choice to the record examining routine.

Non-OPL functions called

BLAR:()

Globals needed

None

Variables used

C% = Check Holds selected menu option.

Customizing

This routine could be eliminated altogether, if you wished, by adding the options 'SEE-TRANSACTIONS' and 'VIEW-S/ORDERS' (or shorter messages!) instead of 'VIEWREC' in the main BANKER menu, and acting accordingly to call `BLAR:(1)` or `BLAR:(2)` depending on the selection. This would make the BANKER menu longer (and less visible), and would save only a few bytes in the final analysis, since two more 'ELSEIF' tests would be needed in Banker.

The Listing

```
BSEE:
LOCAL C%
C%=MENU("RECORDS,S/ORDERS")
IF C%=0         :REM Means cancel operation
  RETURN
ENDIF
BLAR:(C%)       :REM C%=1 or 2
```

4.9 Caption a Transaction Record
BREC:

What it does

This is the routine that adds 'captions' to a transaction-file record, making it easier to understand each line of the record when displayed.

Space required

The space required for the procedure, as listed, but without leading spaces or 'REMarks' (see Chapter 2.1) and excluding space required by any of the non-OPL routines called is:
Source + object code: 449 bytes
Object code only: 224 bytes

How it works

BREC: works in a similar way to SCSEE: (Chapter 3.5). In this procedure, however, a slightly different technique is used, to show that there is more than one way to achieve a desired result! In SCSEE:, a label (AG::) was used to provide the record displaying loop, the test for a jump back to the label being made by an IF statement. In this procedure, the DO...UNTIL technique is used to provide the loop. The saving in object code achieved by using this technique is only 4 bytes, and the saving in source code is about 15 bytes – just 19 bytes altogether.

The top line of a displayed record is prepared from the reference code for the record (i.e., the cheque number or whatever reference you entered), followed by the day and month the entry was made. The next two lines are captioned:

SUM: The amount of the transaction.
BAL: The bank balance resulting from the transaction.

The last line is the description of the transaction, without a caption. All the information is concatenated into S$, before being displayed by a call to the utility SR%:(). Only when a terminating code is returned from SR%: will a return be made to the calling routine: you will recall SR%: enables browsing through the file by pressing the **N**, **B**, **F**, and **L** keys.

Inputs

The transaction file must be current.

Returns

The ASCII value of the **S**, **CLEAR/ON** or **EXE** key, whichever was pressed. This allows the browsing to be terminated, or, if a FIND operation is being undertaken, the next clue-matching record to be found.

Non-OPL functions called

SR%:()

Globals needed

None

Variables used

a) *Field variables*

These hold information from the current record, as follows:
A.R$ = **Reference** The transaction reference
A.DY% = **Day** The day the transaction was made.
A.MN% = **Month** The month the transaction was made.
A.S = **Sum** The amount of the transaction.
A.B = **Balance** The balance following the transaction.
A.D$ = **Details** Details about the transaction.

b) *Local variables*

S$() = **String** To hold all the fields, captions and tab information.
T$() = **Tab** Holds the 'tab' character, which forces a new line in the DISP function.
C% = **Check** Holds the returned value from the SR%:() utility.

Customizing

This routine sets out just one way to display your transaction record: you may wish to tailor the captions and the order of the display to suit your own purposes, bearing in mind that only the top two lines are seen when the record is initially displayed.

The Listing

```
BREC:
LOCAL S$(250),T$(1),C%
T$=CHR$(9)
DO
  S$=A.R$+" ("+NUM$(A.DY%,2)+"/"+
(line continued)       NUM$(A.MN%,2)+")"+T$
  S$=S$+"Sum:"+FIX$(A.S,2,-9)+T$
  S$=S$+"Bal:"+FIX$(A.B,2,-9)+T$
  S$=S$+A.D$
  C%=SR%:(S$)
UNTIL (C%=13) OR (C%=%S) OR (C%=1)
RETURN C%
```

4.10 Caption a S/Order Record
BSSO:

What it does

This procedure adds captions to the Standing Order records, to make them easier to understand when displayed. It is similar to BREC:, in Chapter 4.9 and SCSEE: in Chapter 3.5 – giving yet another example of how a routine can be adapted to suit a specific program requirement.

Space required

The space required for the procedure, as listed, but without leading spaces or 'REMarks' (see Chapter 2.1) and excluding space required by any of the non-OPL routines called is:
Source + object code: 425 bytes
Object code only: 213 bytes

How it works

The principle behind this procedure has already been described (Chapter 3.5). The various fields are concatenated together with captions, to provide a single string variable for display using the SR%:() utility. The first line displays the recipient for the Standing Order, without a caption: the captions used for the next three lines of the display are as follows:

AMOUNT: The amount to be paid each month.
MONTHS LEFT: The number of payments still to be made (hence the number of months left).
LAST PAID: The Month that the last payment was made: this will normally be the current month, since the Standing Orders are updated automatically to the current month each time the program is run. The exception will be when all the payments have been made: the month of the last payment will then be displayed on this line. This field is important in that it enables the program to assess whether or not updating is needed. Note that the MN$:() utility is used to display the name of the month rather than just its 'number'.

As with BREC:, this routine continues calling SR%:(), to display the Standing Order record, until S, **CLEAR/ON** or **EXE** is pressed. SR%:() allows the selection of other records in the file.

Inputs

None. The Standing Order file must be current, of course.

Returns

The ASCII value of the S, **CLEAR/ON** or **EXE** key, whichever was pressed. This allows the browsing to be terminated, or, if a FIND operation is being undertaken, the next clue-matching record to be found.

Non-OPL functions called

MN$:()
SR%:()

Globals needed

None.

Variables used

a) *Field variables*

B.I$ = Item The recipient for the Standing Order.
B.A = Amount The monthly amount of the Standing Order.
B.NOP% = Number Of Payments The number of payments still to be made.
B.PM% = Payment Month The month that the last payment was made.

b) *Local variables*

S$ = String Holds the concatenated field data and caption information.
T$() = Tab Holds the 'tab' character to mark the end of a line for the DISP command.
C% = Check Holds the return value resulting from the call to SR%:().

Customizing

As with the other 'captioning' procedures, you will probably want to use your own captions, and possibly change the order of the displayed lines. You may feel, too, that displaying the 'month of the last payment' is a little superfluous, since whilst payments are due this will always be the current month. It can be useful to know, however, when a final payment was made. In any event, the field is needed by the program to determine whether or not another payment is due – so don't delete the field!

The Listing

```
BSSO:
LOCAL S$(250),T$(1),C%
T$=CHR$(9)
DO
  S$=B.I$+T$+"Amount: "+FIX$(B.A,2,8)+T$
  S$=S$+"Months left:"+NUM$(B.NOP%,3)+T$
  S$=S$+"Last Paid: "+MN$:(B.PM%)
  C%=SR%:(S$)
UNTIL (C%=13) OR (C%=%S) OR (C%=1)
RETURN C%
```

4.11 Make a Transaction
BUPD:

What it does

We now come to the routine that adds a new transaction record to the transaction file. The transaction can be either a debit or a credit. On the face of it, two updating routines could be required, one for credits and one for debits. However, the information required for each type of record is very similar, the only difference between the two actions being that a credit will be added to the current balance, while a debit will be subtracted. The actual information is therefore obtained by a call to another routine (BCAD:(), described in the next Chapter)

This routine allows Credit and Debit transactions to be made without having to return to the main menu, since it is likely that you would want to make a number of entries at the same time.

Space required

The space required for the procedure, as listed, but without leading spaces or 'REMarks' (see Chapter 2.1) and excluding space required by any of the non-OPL routines called is:
Source + object code: 404 bytes
Object code only: 194 bytes

How it works

The last record in the transaction file is made current (we need the latest Bank Balance, which is in the last record), and then a WHILE ...ENDWH loop is used to provide the updates. The choice of Debit or Credit (or 'End') is made from a menu, and an appropriate call made to BCAD:() depending on the choice. Note that the variable C% is given a value of '1' before the loop is entered: if this weren't done, it would have the value '0', and the WHILE C% test would cause an immediate jump through to the end of the procedure – without giving you a chance to update anything!

BCAD:() requires a string argument – either 'CREDIT' or 'DEBIT' – so that an appropriate message can be displayed during the actual input. BCAD:() will update the relevant field information directly, and will also return either a '1' or a '0'. If a '0' is returned, it means an input has been received. If a '1' is returned, it means that the transaction has been 'cancelled' – that is, no reference has been given, or the transaction value is 0. In this circumstance, a jump is made back to the menu (via ENDIF and ENDWH), to allow further selection.

If BCAD:() returns '0', it is assumed a transaction has been satisfactorily entered, and the appropriate adjustment is made to the 'Bank Balance' field, A.B, before the transaction record is APPENDed to the file. The menu loop continues until the CLEAR/ON key is pressed, or 'END' is selected.

Inputs

None.

Returns

Record(s) added to the transaction file.

Non-OPL functions called

BCAD:()

Globals needed

None

Variables used

a) *Field variables*

A.B = Balance The Current Bank balance
A.S = Sum The sum involved in the transaction.

b) *Local variables*

C% = Choice Holds the result of the menu selection.

The Listing

```
BUPD:
LOCAL C%
C%=1
USE A
LAST
WHILE C%
  C%=MENU("DEBIT,CREDIT,END")
  IF C%=1
    IF BCAD:("DEBIT")
      CONTINUE     :REM Means no input
    ENDIF
    A.B=A.B-A.S
  ELSEIF C%=2
    IF BCAD:("CREDIT")
      CONTINUE      :REM Means no input
    ENDIF
      A.B=A.B+A.S
  ELSE RETURN
  ENDIF
  APPEND
ENDWH
```

4.12 Get the Transaction Details

BCAD:()

What it does

The type of information required for a Credit transaction is essentially the same as that for a Debit. This procedure obtains the information required. It has an input argument to identify (for the user) the type of transaction being recorded.

Space required

The space required for the procedure, as listed, but without leading spaces or 'REMarks' (see Chapter 2.1) and excluding space required by any of the non-OPL routines called is:
Source + object code: 401 bytes
Object code only: 213 bytes

How it works

This routine uses the utility `GI$:()` to get the required information from the keyboard. The Reference for the transaction is requested first: this is expected to be an alphanumeric input, so for 'numbers', the **SHIFT** key must be pressed.

If the **EXE** key is pressed without an entry being made, the procedure terminates and returns a '1' to the calling routine, indicating 'no entry' and hence cancelling the transaction record. The sum involved in the transaction is then requested, using the input argument string to indicate the type of transaction. Another opportunity is given to cancel the compete entry at this point: if **EXE** is pressed or '0' is entered, the procedure terminates as before. Otherwise, the details of the transaction are obtained, and then the current date is added to the record by a call to `BRD:`.

Inputs

An input string argument, either 'CREDIT' or 'DEBIT', to indicate the type of transaction being undertaken.

Returns

'0' if the transaction is to be saved as a record.
'1' if the transaction is to be cancelled.

Non-OPL functions called

GI$:()
BRD:

Globals needed

None

Variables used

a) *Field variables*

A.R$ = Reference The reference for the transaction.
A.S = Sum The amount involved in the transaction.
A.D$ = Details Information about the transaction.

b) *Input argument*

M$ = Message Either 'CREDIT' or 'DEBIT', to indicate the type of transaction being undertaken.

Customizing

As with other procedures of this type, you may wish to prune or change the messages. Also you may consider that it is it unnecessary to include two 'escape' routes in the routine – in which case one of the 'IF...ENDIF' tests can be deleted. The message calling for the Reference to be entered could incorporate M$, if you wished. For example:

```
A.R$=GI$:(M$+" Reference",2)
```

would display 'CREDIT Reference' or 'DEBIT Reference', depending on the type of transaction in hand.

The Listing

```
BCAD:(M$)
A.R$=GI$:("Reference (e.g Cheque No. or
(line continued)        SALary)",2)
IF A.R$=""
  RETURN 1      :REM For BUPD's test
ENDIF
A.S=VAL(GI$:("Amount to "+M$,0))
IF A.S=0
  RETURN 1      :REM For BUPD's test
ENDIF
A.D$=GI$:("Brief Details",2)
BRD:
RETURN 0
```

4.13 Change Standing Orders
BASO:

What it does

From time to time it will be necessary to add a new Standing Order, or to change or delete an existing Standing Order. This is the routine that handles the tasks involved.

Space required

The space required for the procedure, as listed, but without leading spaces or 'REMarks' (see Chapter 2.1) and excluding space required by any of the non-OPL routines called is:
Source + object code: 809 bytes
Object code only: 407 bytes

How it works

The Standing Order file is made current, and then the user is presented with a menu of options. These are contained within a DO..UNTIL loop, so that the procedure continues to present options until 'END' is selected from the menu, or the **CLEAR/ON** key is pressed.

The first option – to 'ADD' a new Standing Order – simply involves a call to the BANKER routine BNSO: (described in Chapter 4.5). The 'CHANGE' option follows a similar process to the 'SCUD:' procedure discussed in Chapter 3.6. A message is displayed to inform the user to select the required Standing Order, and then a call is made to the record-locating routine 'BLAR:(2)' (the '2' indicates that the Standing Order file is to be used). Once the required record has been made current, a further DO...UNTIL loop is used to enable any or all of the specific fields to be edited. Selection is by menu, and the editing is achieved using the utilities specially developed for the purpose in Chapter 2. Once editing is complete (C% = 0), the record is re-written to the file (using OPL's UPDATE command).

When 'DELETE' is selected, the required record is selected (using BLAR:(2)) and confirmation is requested that the Standing Order record is in fact to be deleted. This is achieved by displaying the message 'Delete' followed by the first few characters of the 'recipient' field, and then making a call to the YORN%: utility. If the deletion is confirmed (i.e., YORN%: returns a '1') then the deletion is made.

Inputs

None

Returns

None.

Non-OPL functions called

a) *File-handling utilities*

MSG:()
EF:
EI%:
ES$:
YORN%:

b) *Banker Specific procedures*

BNSO:
BLAR:(2)

Globals needed

None.

Variables used

a) *Field variables*

B.I$ = Item The recipient for the Standing Order.
B.A = Amount The sum to be paid each month.
B.NOP% = Number of Payments The number of monthly payments still to be made.

b) *Local variables*

C% = Change The selection from the field-to-update menu.
D% = Do The selection from the updating-options menu.

The Listing

```
BASO:
LOCAL C%,D%
USE B
CLS
DO
  D%=MENU("ADD,CHANGE,DELETE,END")
  IF D%=1
    BNSO:
  ELSEIF D%=2
    MSG:("Select S/Order")
    BLAR:(2)
    DO
      C%=MENU("NAME,AMOUNT,MONTHS-LEFT,END")
      IF C%=1
        B.I$=ES$:(B.I$)
      ELSEIF C%=2
        B.A=EF:(B.A,2)
      ELSEIF C%=3
        B.NOP%=EI%:(B.NOP%)
      ELSE C%=0
      ENDIF
    UNTIL C%=0
    UPDATE
  ELSEIF D%=3
    MSG:("Select S/O")
    BLAR:(2)
    PRINT"Delete",LEFT$(B.I$,6);"-"
    IF YORN%:
      ERASE
    ENDIF
  ELSE D%=0
  ENDIF
UNTIL D%=0
```

4.14 Verify Bank Statement
BCBS:

What it does

This procedure helps to simplify that tedious task of comparing what the Bank thinks we have spent against what we know we have spent. (Or vice versa). To use the procedure, one should first of all go through every transaction record in turn, ticking them off on the Bank Statement. The amounts involved in each Credit and Debit that does not appear on the Bank Statement should be listed separately. This procedure is then selected from the main Banker menu ('VERIFY'), and the Debits entered one by one as requested, ending by entering '0' (zero). The Credits are then entered as requested, again ending by entering a '0'. You will then be prompted to enter the bottom line of the Bank Statement (the Bank's balance), and the procedure makes the necessary adjustments to show that, with any luck, the Bank agrees with your records. Otherwise, the procedure calculates who is kidding who.

Space required

The space required for the procedure, as listed, but without leading spaces or 'REMarks' (see Chapter 2.1) and excluding space required by any of the non-OPL routines called is:
Source + object code: 917 bytes
Object code only: 465 bytes

How it works

The Credits and Debits are each entered within a DO...UNTIL loop, the 'UNTIL' being a '0' entry. The utility GI$:() is used to obtain the entries, with a message that incorporates the entry number. The Bank Balance figure is then obtained, and this is adjusted by deducting the Debits and adding the Credits that have not yet reached the bank. The resulting figure should, of course, tally with the balance given in the last record of the transaction file.

The difference (if any) between the Bank Statement and your own records is converted to a string, and then this is built into a message for display on the screen, indicating 'Balance' or the nature of the error.

Inputs

None.

Returns

None.

Non-OPL functions called

GI$:()

Globals needed

None

Variables used

a) *Field Variables*

A.B = Balance The Bank Balance according to the last record in the transaction file.

b) *Local variables*

C = Credit Accumulator for the total amount of Credits not on the Bank Statement.

D = Debit Accumulator for the total amount of Debits not on the Bank Statement.

T = Temporary Holds the input value

I% = Item Counter for the number of Credits or Debits that have been entered.

R = Reconcile The calculated value of the Bank balance adjusted for non-received Credits and Debits.

S$ = String Holds the string to display the result of the verification.

Customizing

You may consider it unnecessary to have a count of the input items – in which case all the code related to 'I%' can be removed.

The Listing

```
BCBS:
LOCAL C,D,T,I%,R,S$(24)
I%=1
DO
  T=VAL(GI$:("Enter DEBIT No "+NUM$(I%,2)+
(line continued)   " NOT on Statement",0))
  D=D+T
  I%=I%+1
UNTIL T=0
I%=1
DO
  T=VAL(GI$:("CREDIT No "+NUM$(I%,2)+
(line continued)   " NOT on Statement",0))
  C=C+T
  I%=I%+1
UNTIL T=0
CLS
T=VAL(GI$:("ENTER BANK BALANCE ON STATEMENT:",0))
CLS
USE A
LAST
R=T-D+C
S$=FIX$(ABS(A.B-R),2,8)
IF R<A.B
  S$=S$+" MORE than"
ELSEIF R>A.B
  S$=S$+" LESS than"
ELSE
  S$="BALANCE with"
ENDIF
VIEW(1,"Records show "+S$+" Bank statement")
```

4.15 Print Out Banker Records

BPRO:

What it does

This final routine in the BANKER suite provides a tabulated print-out of the Standing Orders and transaction records. It is assumed, of course, that you have a printer and the Psion Comms Link (or the earlier RS232 interface).

Space required

The space required for the procedure, as listed, but without leading spaces or 'REMarks' (see Chapter 2.1) and excluding space required by any of the non-OPL routines called is:
Source + object code: 950 bytes
Object code only: 436 bytes

How it works

The print-out is in two parts. First, the Standing Order file is made current, suitable headings are printed, and then each Standing Order record is printed out in a formatted way, so that everything lines up neatly. The numeric 'Month Last Paid' information is converted to a three-letter name abbreviation, by a call to the utility `MN$:()`.

Then the transaction file is made current, suitable headings are printed for the transaction file, and all of the transaction records printed out in a neat tabular form. The utility `FIL$:()` is used to add spaces to record fields which may be under-length, and to help keep the columns lined up. Note that for print-out, each transaction date is converted to the form '10 JAN 88', and that the sequence is 'DATE, REF, AMOUNT, DETAILS, BALANCE'.

Inputs

None.

Returns

None.

Non-OPL functions called

FIL$:()
MN$:()

Globals needed

None.

Variables used

a) *Transaction-file Field Variables*

A.DY% = Day The day the transaction was made.
A.MN% = Month The month (number) that the transaction was made.
A.Y% = Year The year that the transaction was made. (Note that only the last two digits are actually printed out).
A.R$ = Reference The user reference for the transaction.
A.S = Sum The sum involved in the transaction.
A.D$ = Details about the transaction.
A.B = Balance The bank balance after the transaction has been made.

b) *Standing Order file field variables*

B.I$ = Item The name of the recipient for the Standing Order.
B.A = Amount The monthly sum to be paid under the Standing Order.
B.NOP% = Number of Payments The number of months/Standing Order payments left.
B.PM% = Paid Month The month the last payment was made.

c) *Local variable*

T$ = Tab Holds the 'tab' character (9), to provide tabular spacing.

Customizing

This routine was written and tested using an Epson™ printer. You may find that the spacing needs adjusting to suit your own printer. You can, of course, change the order of columns, and the way that the information is printed out, to suit your own purposes. This routine, and the similar routine given for the Stock Control program in Chapter 3.9, should enable you to prepare print-out routines for your own file-handling programs. Remember to use semi-colons to keep the print-out of a record on one line.

Another possibility is to embed printer codes in the print-out – to produce bold headings, for example: you will find the codes in the book that comes with your printer. Such refinements have not been used here since they are very printer dependent.

The Listing

```
BPRO:
LOCAL T$(1)
T$=CHR$(9)
USE B
FIRST
LPRINT"STANDING ORDERS"
LPRINT
LPRINT FIL$:("NAME",8);T$;" AMOUNT    ";
(line continued)        T$;"NOP";T$;"LAST PAID"
DO
  LPRINT FIL$:(B.I$,8);T$;FIX$(B.A,2,-9);
(line continued)        T$;NUM$(B.NOP%,-3);T$;
  LPRINT MN$:(B.PM%)
  NEXT
UNTIL EOF
LPRINT
LPRINT
USE A
FIRST
LPRINT"RECORDS"
LPRINT"DATE     ";T$;"REF ";T$;"  AMOUNT    ";T$;
(line continued)          "DETAILS ";T$;" BALANCE"
DO
  LPRINT NUM$(A.DY%,2);" ";MN$:(A.MN%);
  LPRINT" ";RIGHT$(NUM$(A.YR%,4),2);T$;
  LPRINT A.R$;T$;FIX$(A.S,2,-8);
(line continued)          T$;FIL$:(A.D$,15);
  LPRINT FIX$(A.B,2,-8)
  NEXT
UNTIL EOF
```

CHAPTER 5

General Programs

5.1 Pot-Pourri

Something for everyone?

In this Chapter of the book you'll find a small mixture of quite different programs and routines. For the most part, they represent typical 'quick solutions' to problems: only one program took longer than 30 minutes to develop, write and 'debug'. The object of including the programs in this book is not so much to provide useful utilities (which they may or may not do, depending on your own particular needs), but to give further examples of how programs can be prepared for Organiser, and how its use can thus be extended and tailored to do what *you* want.

Where most other types of 'programmable' computer – particularly the domestic 'home computers' – have a plethora of magazines providing program listings for the keen user to enter, the Psion Organiser, perhaps surprisingly, has very few sources of listings. This is unfortunate, for entering routines that others have written (and then adapting and even improving on them) is an excellent way for beginners to learn about the programming language.

All too often, the newcomer to computing feels frustrated by not knowing quite where to start writing the program he or she wants. In many instances, the reason is because the programs they want are too ambitious for them to tackle as 'first' programs. File handling programs are a good example of this. As you will appreciate from the earlier Chapters of this book, a considerable amount of planning (as well as programming) goes into a preparing routines to handle files. They call for a certain amount of programming experience (but not necessarily *expertise*), particularly if the best use is to be made of the available memory space.

Start small

The secret for budding programmers is simple: start with short routines – even 'one-liners'. In the main, one-line routines are used to perform simple mathematical calculations or conversions. For example, suppose you are on holiday, and you wish to convert the cost of items in the foreign currency to English money. Knowing that the exchange rate is (say) 250 foreign coins to the pound, you could use Organiser's CALCulator mode to work out every conversion individually – first entering the foreign cost, then dividing it by 250. At least with Organiser, you won't have to keep re-entering the 'divide by 250' bit to make repeated calculations.

Alternatively, you could write a very short 'function' on the Organiser (for use in the calculator mode). For the above exchange rate example, this could look something like:

```
CONV:(P)
RETURN P/250
```

In the CALCulator mode of Organiser, one would use this function by entering the foreign cost within the brackets. Thus, if the cost were 478 in the foreign currency, you would enter:

```
CALC:CONV:(478)
```

This is fine – until the exchange rate changes. You may then say to yourself "Wouldn't it be handy if I could change the exchange rate without having to fiddle about with the program source code in order to amend it." Having spoken to youself in such a manner, you may then extend the one-line routine to allow the exchange rate to 'stay' in memory when the Organiser is switched off, and to cope with different exchange rates. You could add a few messages, a 'menu' perhaps – and suddenly, you have a facility which is more practical, and which is a 'program' rather than a function, so it can be added to the main menu that appears when you switch on as another option. (A function – or a procedure that needs an argument input within brackets – must be 'called' from another program or run from the calculator: it cannot be run from the main menu). The first program in this Chapter provides a short Exchange rate program, capable of further expansion.

Other programs will help you to determine the date of Easter Sunday for any year you care to choose, the umpteenth root of a number, how many miles per gallon your car is giving you (even though you fill it with 'litres'!), the state of your 'Biorhythms' on any given date, how many days there are between two dates, and what the date is a given number of days after (or before) another date, and so on.

Hopefully, they will inspire you to create your own routines, so that you can maximise the use of your Organiser.

5.2 Exchange Rates

EXCH:

What it does

Here is a fairly simple program to convert the cost of goods priced in foreign currencies to good old pounds sterling – a useful routine to have when travelling abroad. The program is 'menu' driven when run, you have the choice of making an exchange calculation, checking the current exchange rate you're using, or entering a new exchange rate. Pressing the **CLEAR/ON** key from the menu stops the program from running. You can also exit the program by entering '0' or simply pressing the **EXE** key when asked for the 'FOREIGN COST'.

Space required

The space required for the procedure, as listed, but without leading spaces or 'REMarks' (see Chapter 2.1) and excluding space required by any of the non-OPL routines called is:
Source + object code: 630 bytes
Object code only: 295 bytes

How it works

The program uses the utility `GI$:()`, developed in Chapter 2, to get in the cost and the exchange rate information.

The 'problem' with storing an exchange rate is – where do you store it? One method would be to put it into a file, but the programming and space needed to have a file with just one piece of information in it is quite unjustified, especially as there is an alternative – provided you don't mind 'forfeiting' one of the CALCulator's memories. In this program, calculator memory 'M9' is used to store the exchange rate. As you know, the calculator memories retain their information even when Organiser is 'switched off'.

The program starts by assigning the menu-choice variable (C%) to the value '1', so enabling the menu to be used as often as required within a WHILE...ENDWH loop, until the **CLEAR/ON** key is pressed. The 'NEWRATE' routine (option '2') starts by assigning to M9 the result of the input obtained via the utility GI$:(). (Notice how an assignment to a calculator memory can be made directly). It is assumed that, having entered a new exchange rate, you will want to 'test' it out immediately: hence the second part of the routine for this option is, in fact, the routine to obtain the foreign cost and to convert it using the exchange rate. If the menu option 'EXCH' is selected (option '1'), a jump is made to this part of the routine.

The conversion to pound sterling involves dividing the cost in foreign currency by the exchange rate. If no exchange rate has been entered, M9 will contain '0' - and a **DIVIDE BY ZERO** error will occur. One could use the OPL language's error-trapping commands to prevent the error stopping the program from running: in the procedure given here, a simple test is made on the value of M9 before the foreign cost is entered and a calculation is made. (Testing before a cost is entered saves wasting time making the entry). If '0' is entered as the foreign cost (or the **EXE** key is pressed), the program is terminated. There are thus two ways to end the program – always a good technique, in case you forget one of them!

The messages and exchanges are displayed on the screen using OPL's VIEW function, which keeps the display visible on the screen until any key is pressed. The alternative is to use the PRINT and GET commands. The exchange calculations are formatted using OPL's FIX$ function, truncating the answer to two decimal places.

Using EXCH

This program can be RUN from Organiser's PROGramming menu, or it can be installed as an option on the main menu that appears when Organiser is switched on. To do this, you place the 'cursor' at the place you want the option to appear in the menu, then press the **MODE** key. Organiser will respond with the message 'INSERT ITEM': you then simply type in the name of the program 'EXCH'.

Non-OPL functions called

GI$:

Variables used

a) *Local*

F = Foreign cost

C% = Choice Holds the menu selection.

P$ = Pound Holds a character not unlike the '£' sign.

b) *'Permanent'*

M9 = Calculator memory 9 Holds the exchange rate. The data is retained in memory after Organiser has been 'switched off'.

Customizing

There's plenty of scope here for the intrepid traveller to extend the program, by adding in a selection of exchange rates – each held in a different CALCulator memory, perhaps, or if there is a large number of rates, in a file – with menu selection of the required rate.

The Listing

```
EXCH:
LOCAL F,C%,P$(1)
P$=CHR$(237)        :REM Set up Pound character
C%=1
WHILE C%
  C%=MENU("EXCH,NEWRATE,SEERATE")
  IF C%=1
    GOTO EX::
  ELSEIF C%=2
    M9=VAL(GI$:("RATE TO THE "+P$,0)
EX::
CLS
    IF M9=0
      VIEW(2,"NO EXCHANGE RATE")
      CONTINUE
    ENDIF
F=VAL(GI$:("FOREIGN COST",0))
    IF F=0
      RETURN
    ENDIF
    C%=VIEW(2,"="+P$+FIX$(F/M9,2,8))
  ELSEIF C%=3
    VIEW(2,"RATE="+FIX$(M9,2,8))
  ENDIF
ENDWH
```

5.3 Miles per Gallon
MPG:

What it does

The habit of calculating miles per gallon stays with us, even though the pumps insist on pouring litres into our tanks. This program shows how easy it is to have Organiser make all the necessary calculations for you – and to prompt you for the information it needs.

Space required

The space required for the procedure, as listed, but without leading spaces or 'REMarks' (see Chapter 2.1) is:
Source + object code: 279 bytes
Object code only: 128 bytes

How it works

This simple procedure is typical of the way that Organiser can be programmed to handle calculations, and to prompt you for all the information it requires. 'CHR$(63)' on the PRINT lines requesting information holds the '?' character. Once the necessary information has been entered, the answer is calculated, FIXed to two decimal places, and printed – all in one program line. The 'clear screen' (CLS) commands prevent the display from scrolling untidily.

Using MPG

This program can be RUN from Organiser's PROGramming menu, or it can be installed as an option on the main menu that appears when Organiser is switched on. To do this, you place the 'cursor' at the place you want the option to appear in the menu, then press the **MODE** key. Organiser will respond with the message 'INSERT ITEM' – you then simply type in the name of the program 'MPG'.

Non-OPL functions called

None

Variables used

L = Litres The number of litres, to be converted to gallons.
M = Miles

Customizing

This program is fairly trivial and can, of course, be modified. Its main purpose is to give you a basis for writing routines that can handle the calculations you need. The first step is to set down the formula: for example, to work out the Miles Per Gallon from the number of litres of petrol and the number of miles, the calculation would be:

$$\frac{\text{Miles}}{\text{Litres x } 0.22}$$

Your routine must arrange to get in the 'unknown' parts – the Miles and Litres, in this instance – with prompts to help the user, and then make the necessary calculation. Even the most complex formulae can be adapted quite easily.

If you have entered the utility 'GI$:()', you could use it in place of each set of 'PRINT..., INPUT..., and CLS statements to get in the necessary information.

The Listing

```
MPG:
LOCAL L,M
PRINT"No OF LITRES";CHR$(63)
INPUT L
CLS
PRINT"HOW MANY MILES";CHR$(63)
INPUT M
CLS
PRINT"MILES PER GAL="
PRINT FIX$(M/(L*.22),2,8)
GET   :REM Otherwise the display will clear.
```

5.4 Umpteenth Roots

ROOTD:, ROOT:()

What it does

A number of people have enquired why Organiser II doesn't have a function for calculating the *n*th root of a number. As with any other 'missing' function – it is fairly easy to add what you want. Here is a program and a function to perform the task: the function allows for the number of decimal places in the answer to be specified.

Space required

The space required for the procedures, as listed is:

a) *The program, ROOTD:*
Source + object code: 236 bytes
Object code only: 111 bytes

b) *The function, ROOT:()*
Source + object code: 102 bytes
Object code only: 57 bytes

How it works

A mathematical way of writing the nth root is

$$X^{1/n}$$

which can be expressed in Organiser's terms as

X**(1/N)

or, in English, "X raised to the power of: '1' divided by 'N' ". This is the 'formula' used by both the program and the function to calculate the required root. The program 'prompts' for the information, then displays the answer. This can be installed on the main menu if you wish. The function must be called from another routine, or used from Organiser's CALCulator mode. It requires three input parameters: the base number, the required root, and the number of decimal places for the answer.

Example of use

The function ROOT:() must be used from the CALCulator mode:

```
CALC:ROOT:(64,6,1)
```

or 'called' from another program:

```
R=ROOT:(X,N,3)
```

ROOTD: can be RUN from the PROGramming menu of Organiser.

Non-OPL functions called

None

Variables used

N = Number
R = Root
D = Decimal The number of decimal places.

The Listings

a) *The program*

```
ROOTD:
LOCAL N,R
PRINT"NUMBER="
INPUT N
CLS
PRINT"ROOT="
INPUT R
CLS
PRINT R;" ROOT OF ";N
PRINT "=";FIX$(N**(1/R)),4,10)
GET
```

b) *The function*

```
ROOT:(N,R,D)
RETURN VAL(FIX$(N**(1/R),D,10))
```

5.5 Number 'base' Conversion

NUMCON:, BASE:()

What it does

This program of two procedures is included to demonstrate a programming technique known as 'recursion'. Recursion is when a procedure calls itself – and continues calling itself until a condition is met. In this program, the procedure 'BASE:()' is recursive, and is used to find the value of a number in a different base (to a maximum of 'base 16').

The base of the number is, in effect, the first value that requires 'double figures' to represent a value. Thus in the decimal system, the base is '10' since it needs two digits to represent the value '10'. As examples of the conversion, the decimal value '9' (9 to the base 10) is '10' in octal (base 8), and the decimal value '32' (32 to the base '10') is '20' in hexadecimal (20 to the base '16').

What use are numbering systems to different 'bases'? Computers operate on a binary system – numbers to the base '2' – and use also a numbering system that's to a base '8' (octal) or '16' (hexadecimal). Converting from one system to another is a frequent requirement. This program provides conversions from the decimal system to any base up to '16', but as mentioned previously, its main purpose is to demonstrate the recursion technique.

Space required

The space required for the procedures as listed, but without leading spaces, is:

a) *Numcon*
Source + object code: 458 bytes
Object code only: 219 bytes

b) *Base*
Source + object code: 278 bytes
Object code only: 144 bytes

Both procedures are requires for the program to run

How they work

When numbers have a base greater than '9', it is necessary to allocate a 'symbol' to the values 10, 11, 12 ... and so on. In hexadecimal (base 16), for example, the values 10, 11, 12, 13 ... 15 are represented by the letters A, B, C ... F. The main procedure, NUMCON, sets up an array of numbers and letters to represent values up to 15. When a value is required, the appropriate array element is selected and printed. For example, the 3rd element in the array contains '3', and the 12th element in the array contains the character 'C'.

Once the array has been initialised, you are prompted for the decimal number to be converted, then you are prompted for the required base. The conversion and print-out is made by a call to `BASE:()`.

One way to find the representation of a number in a different base is to divide that number by the base repeatedly, then to take all the remainders in reverse order. Thus, to convert decimal '13' to binary (base 2):

13	divided by 2	=	6	remainder **1**
6	divided by 2	=	3	remainder **0**
3	divided by 2	=	1	remainder **1**
1	divided by 2	=	0	remainder **1**

Taking the remainders in reverse order, the binary equivalent of decimal 13 is '**1101**'. The procedure '`BASE:()`' performs this task using the recursive technique. First of all, the sign of the number is assessed. If it is negative, then a '–' is printed. The value of the number is then made 'positive', and `BASE:()` is called again. Because the procedure `BASE:()` is called again, it is stored again in RAM. The dividing process then begins: if the number is still greater than the base, the procedure `BASE:()` is called yet again (placed in RAM again), but this time using the divided value as the argument. This process is repeated until the 'end of the line' is reached – the number is no longer greater than the base (N% is no longer greater than B%). In the last copy of the procedure in RAM, processing jumps to the last '`ELSE PRINT A$(N%+1)`' statement – to print the character corresponding to the *last* remainder. Then processing returns to the line following the `BASE:()` call in the *preceding* procedure stored in RAM, to print the character corresponding to the next remainder. In other words, the remainders are printed out in reverse order.

This technique keeps the actual length of the procedure very short for storage purposes. When run however, there will be as many copies of the procedure in RAM as the are 'recursions'. But these do not remain in RAM, of course, after the program has finished.

Non-OPL functions called

NUMCON: calls BASE:().

Globals needed

The variables required for BASE:() are made Global in NUMCON:.

Variables used

a) *Global*

A$ = Array Holds the characters representing values 1 to 15. Note that the first element of the array is A$(1), which holds the value '0': it is therefore necessary to add '1' to the array index to identify the correct aray element.
N% = Number The number to be converted
B% = Base The new base for the conversion.

b) *Local (to NUMCON:)*

I% = Index For allocating the array elements to values

Customizing

As listed here, the program must be run each time it is required to convert a decimal number to another base. It will be very easy for you to create a loop so that any number of conversions can be made, until the **CLEAR/ON** key is pressed to terminate the routine. You find this technique used extensively throughout this book, and it will be good practice for you to adapt this procedure accordingly.

The Listings

Enter both procedures seperately:

a) *NUMCON* *(continues overleaf)*

```
NUMCON:
GLOBAL A$(17,1),N%,B%
LOCAL I%
I%=0
DO                  :REM Set up the numbers
```

```
  A$(I%+1)=CHR$(I%+48)
  I%=I%+1
UNTIL I%=10
I%=65
DO                :REM Set up the 'letters'
  A$(I%-54)=CHR$(I%)
  I%=I%+1
UNTIL I%=71
CLS       :REM Start a 'loop' here, if wanted
PRINT "NUMBER:";
INPUT N%
CLS
PRINT "BASE:";
INPUT B%
CLS
PRINT N%;" TO BASE ";B%
BASE:(N%,B%)
GET
```

b) *BASE*

```
BASE:(N%,B%)
IF N%<0
  PRINT "-";        :REM Negative number-print'-'
  BASE:(-N%,B%)    :REM and make N% 'positive'
ELSEIF N%>=B%
  BASE:(N%/B%,B%)
  PRINT A$(N%-((N%/B%)*B%)+1);  :REM Semi colons
ELSE PRINT A$(N%+1);            :REM important
ENDIF
```

5.6 Day and Date Finder

DAYFIND:, GTDATE:, FTOD:, DTOF:

What it does

How many times have you wondered what the date will be in a certain number of days time, or what it was a certain number of days ago? Alternatively, how often have you wanted to know how many days there are between two specified dates? You need never wonder again. Enter this program – a suite of four procedures – and you'll have the answers at your fingertips, for any dates between May 1st 1900 and Dec 31st 2099.

The reason for this limitation is that the century years are only leap years if they are divisible by 400, not the usual '4', and the program does not take these century years into account. (As a matter of interest, the Organiser seems to think 1900 was a leap year. Ooops!).

When run, the program offers the two options – to find the number of days-between-dates, or to find the date resulting from adding or subtracting days to a date. Having made either choice, you then enter the start date in the form dd/mm/yyyy (i.e. 27/08/1988). The way the program works, you can enter any month number except zero: for example, you could enter 25/13/1988. The program will translate this to be 23/01/1989. The same thing will happen if you enter too many days for the month: the program will sort out the actual date represented.

If you are finding the number of days between dates, you are then prompted for the second date: this can be a date before or after the first date, it doesn't matter. The number of days between the two dates will be displayed.

If you want to know what the date will be (or was) a certain number of days away from the start date, you will be prompted for that number of days: enter a negative number to find the date before the start date (e.g. entering -21 will find the date three weeks before the start date).

Some unusual techniques have been used in the development of this suite: the conventional approach of having a (large) array containing the number of days in each month has been avoided: the routines used are shorter and faster.

Space required

The space required for the procedures, as listed, but without leading spaces or 'REMarks' (see Chapter 2.1) and excluding space required by any of the non-OPL routines called is:

a) *DAYFIND*
Source + object code: 617 bytes
Object code only: 297 bytes

b) *GTDATE*
Source + object code: 597 bytes
Object code only: 253 bytes

c) *DTOF*
Source + object code: 275 bytes
Object code only: 158 bytes

d) *FTOD*
Source + object code: 662 bytes
Object code only: 363 bytes

How it works

The principle behind this program is very simple: the translation of the principle is perhaps not quite so simple. When a date is entered, it is converted to a 'factor', which is in fact the number of days from 1st Jan 1900 to the entered date (including an erroneous Feb 29th for the year 1900). To find the number of days between two dates, the the 'factor' for the second date is calculated, and then one of the factors is subtracted from the other: provided the dates are between 1/3/1900 and 31/12/2099, the answer will be correct.

Similarly, to find what the date will be (or was) a given number of days from a specified date, the number of days is added (or subtracted) from the 'factor' for the date, and the resulting 'factor' is converted back to a date again.

The procedures involved are DAYFIND:, which is the main controlling routine; GTDATE:, which allows a date to be entered in a fairly easy, user-friendly way; DTOF:, which converts a date to the date-factor; and FTOD:, which converts a date-factor back to a date.

DAYFIND: is fairly straightforward. The option menu is contained within a loop, controlled by a label and a GOTO command. The **CLEAR/ON** key must be pressed to finish using the program. After either of the two menu options has been selected, the first or start date is obtained by a call to GTDATE:(). This is given the argument '1' for message purposes. Then, depending on the option selected, either the second date is entered, or the number of days is entered – preceded by a 'plus' or 'minus' sign to indicate 'after' or 'before' the start date. (Note: When you look at the procedure you'll see that, for the second option, it is only necessary to use 'ELSE', not 'ELSEIF C%=2', since C% must equal 2 if processing reaches this point).

The appropriate calculations are made, and the number of days or the new date (depending on the selected option) is displayed on the screen. For convenience, the month number is converted to the month name, using the utility MN$:() from Chapter 2. Note that whilst the year, month, day and factor are all integer values, floating point variables are used. This is because the remainder resulting from divisions is required in the calculations. For the display printout, therefore, the floating point values are converted to integers – the day (D) and month (M) in DAYFIND:, and the year in FTOD:.

The **GTDATE:()** procedure is probably longer than it need be – but it is designed to be 'user friendly(ish)'. There is always a problem when entering dates – one can choose to enter it one value at a time (PRINT"ENTER YEAR" :INPUT Y, etc). In this procedure, a technique similar to that given in the utility GI$:() is used, so that the entire date can be entered at once, provided it is to a specified format. Why not use GI$:()? You can – but for a string input (which is what is necessary), the keyboard is set to alphanumeric by GI$:(), and that means holding down the **SHIFT** key whilst entering the numbers, with a potential, frustrating error occuring on the first character. All the characters required for a date are numeric (including the day-month-year separators) and hence the GTDATE:() routine sets the keyboard for numeric inputs.

Note that, as written, the day-month-year separators can be any character on the 'numeric' keyboard, not just '/'. The format for the date is included in the displayed prompt as a reminder: it must be in the form dd/mm/yyyy (i.e. 01/09/1988) to enable the actual values required to be 'picked out'. To avoid incorrect entries causing errors, error-trapping is used, with an addition to the displayed message to enter the date 'again'. (Note how the word 'AGAIN' is added only once even if several entries have to be made). Errors can occur elsewhere in the program if a zero is entered for the day, month or year and so a test is made to ensure this hasn't happened. Any number multiplied by zero is zero, so the test involves simply multiplying all three variables for day, month and year together: if the result is zero, at least one of the variables must be zero, and the date must be entered again. (The 'IF X*Y*Z' line in the procedure means 'if the three variables multiplied together have a value other than zero', and is much shorter than 'IF (X=0) OR (Y=0) OR (Z=0)')

DTOF: converts the date to a value representing the number of days between that date and Jan 1st 1900 (with the extra day for the non existing Feb 29 in that year). First, 1900 is subtracted from the entered year, to give a two-digit number. Then comes a little sum – every year is assumed (initially) to have 365 days, and every month is assumed (initially) to have 31 days. The calculation is

(365 x years) + (31 x days-to-preceding-month) + (day of the month).

The 'factor' value obtained so far obviously needs to be corrected. If the month number is 'less than three' (i.e. January or February), we need to add a day for every leap year up to the *preceding* year. This is done by adding to the 'factor' the 'integer of (years-1) divided by four'. For the months 3 to 12, the *current* year must be taken into account when testing for a leap year.

Now, what about the months – we started by assuming every one of them has 31 days. For January and February, there is no problem: if the month is January, there is no preceding month in that year (and 31 x 0 = 0), and if it is February, then the preceding month – January – indeed does have 31 days. So for these two months, no correction is needed.

If we look at the error incurred by the assumption each month has 31 days, we see that over the months the error accumulates as follows: days to March and April will each be 3 days out, to May and June four days out, to July, August and September five days out, to October and November six days out, and to the beginning of December, seven days out. Those of you who remember your school days, (algebra, graphs and all that), will be able to plot these values on a graph and deduce the equation of a line which can be passed through each of the integer values. To save you getting your pencils, paper and thinking caps out, the correction factor line is defined by:

$$X=0.4Y+2.3$$

So, all we need to do to find the correction factor for any month is to multiply the month number by 0.4, add 2.3, and forget the decimal bit. (Try it with July – month 7, for example. 7x0.4 is 2.8, adding on 2.3 gives us 5.1, forgetting the decimal bit leaves us with 5, the number to be deducted to make our factor correct for the days to the beginning of July). All of which makes for a procedure that's much shorter and a much faster running than having an array of months and days to run through.

The **FTOD:** procedure requires similar tricks to convert the factor number back to a date: it would be pointless being able to produce the factor number without having an array of months, if an array of months is needed to convert it back again. The first item to derive from the factor is the year. If we look at the number of days in four years, and divide that by four, we get 365.25. Consequently, dividing the factor number by 365.25 – and again, ignoring the decimal bits (i.e. taking the integer of the result) – gives us the year.

We next need to find how many days are left, to be allocated out to months and days. This is achieved by using a utility we developed in Chapter 2, called 'MOD:()', to find the remainder from dividing the factor number by 365.25. We also need to know whether or not the year just calculated is a leap year: again, MOD:() will give us the answer: if there is no remainder when the year is divided by 4, it is a leap year (pity aboput 1900). If it is a leap year, then the number of days in January and February is 59. Otherwise it's 58.

The next step is to see whether the number of days in the year is less than the number of days in January and February. If it is, we can quickly arrive at the month and date answer. Suppose the number of days is 35: the integer result of dividing by 31 (the number of days in January) is 1, to which we add one to make '2', for February. If the number of days is less than 31, the integer result of dividing by 31 is 0 – to which adding one gives '1', for January. The integer remainder resulting from dividing the number of days by 31, plus one, similarly gives the day of the month for the first two months.

Notice, incidentally, that the `MOD:()` utility needs two floating point arguments: hence the use of the decimal point in the actual values entered as arguments.

How do we determine how many days are in each month for the rest of the year without an array? If we say that every month has 30 days, have a look at the pattern of days that need to be added to correct for the '31' day months:

March	0	August
April	1	September
May	0	October
June	1	November
July	0	December

We can use this regular pattern to make the calculations, by repeated 'deductions', in two nested loops. First of all, the number of days in January and February are deducted. Then, a loop to deduct 30, 31, 30, 31 and 30 days is repeated twice. When the number of days left becomes negative, we know we have 'gone too far'. It is then a simple matter to add back the number of days for the month to get the actual day. And to find out which month it is, we simply add in the current position within the inner loop – and add five if the outer loop has been completed once. Again, the process requires considerably less space than would be needed if an array were used.

Non-OPL functions called

a) *DAYFIND*

GTDATE:()
DTOF:
FTOD:
GI$:() (Utility)
MN$:() (Utility)

b) *GTDATE*

None.

c) *DTOF*

None.

d) *FTOD*

MOD:() (Utility)

Globals needed

All the procedures use the Globals declared in the main DAYFIND: routine, namely:
Y = Year
M = Month
D = Day
F = Factor

Variables used

Apart from the Globals mentioned above, the variables used by the procedures are as follows.

a) *DAYFIND*
C% = Choice Holds the menu selection.
F1 = Factor 1 The factor number for the first date.
F2 = Factor 2 The factor number for the second date.

b) *GTDATE*
M$ = Message Holds part of the date prompt message
D$ = Date Holds the input date
C% = Check Holds the first character of the date input.

c) *DTOF*
F = Factor

d) *FTOD*
JF% = JanFeb Holds the number of days in January and February
C = Counter 1 Outer loop counter
K = Counter 2 Inner loop counter
E% = Extra day Holds the value of the 'extra day' factor.
ND = Number of Days Holds the number of days (left) in the current year

Customizing

The GTDATE:() routine could be shortened, if you are prepared to use a simpler 'entry' system to obtain the date. Do ensure, whatever system you use, that the year, month and day are allocated to the Global variables Y, M and D, and that the year is a 4-digit number. Be careful about adapting the FTOD: and DTOF: routines: even minor changes to these could seriously affect the accuracy of the results.

There is another routine which could be added very easily to this suite: a 'day-of-the-week' routine. Since days run consecutively (brilliant observation), one has only to subtract one from the factor number for the required date (to allow for that 29/Feb/1900!), and to find the remainder resulting from dividing the answer by 7. It would then be a simple matter to convert the number so obtained (0 to 6) into a day of the week: you could use a routine similar to the utility `MN$:()`. However, do remember that, even though it may be slower, you could find the information by using Organiser's Diary...

The Listings

All four procedures must be entered separately.

a) *DAYFIND*

```
DAYFIND:
GLOBAL Y,M,D,F
LOCAL C%,F1,F2
AG::
C%=MENU("No-of-days,Date+days")
IF C%              :REM If C%=0, CLEAR/ON was pressed
  GTDATE:(1)
  F1=DTOF:         :REM Get the start date
    IF C%=1
       GTDATE:(2)
       F2=DTOF:
       CLS
        PRINT"Date 1 to Date 2=";
        PRINT ABS(F2-F1);" Days"
       ELSE
        F=F1+VAL(GI$:("Days (+ or -)",0))
       FTOD:
       CLS
        PRINT"Date is"
         PRINT INT(D);"/";MN$:(INT(M));"/";Y+1900
    ENDIF
    GET
    GOTO AG::
ENDIF
```

b) *GTDATE*

```
GTDATE:(N%)
LOCAL M$(7),D$(10),C%
IF N%=1
  M$="1"
  ELSE
  M$="2"
ENDIF
KSTAT 3
AG::
CLS
C%=VIEW(1,"Enter DATE "+M$+" as DD/MM/YYYY")
AT 1,2
PRINT CHR$(C%);
INPUT D$
D$=CHR$(C%)+D$
ONERR ER::
Y=VAL(RIGHT$(D$,4))
M=VAL(MID$(D$,4,2))
D=VAL(LEFT$(D$,2))
IF Y*M*D
  KSTAT 1
  RETURN
  ELSE
  GOTO ER::
ENDIF

ER::
IF LEN(M$)=1
  M$=M$+" AGAIN"
  ENDIF
GOTO AG::
```

c) *DTOF* *(continues overleaf)*

```
DTOF:
LOCAL F
Y=Y-1900
F=(365*Y)+D+31*(M-1)
IF M<3
   F=F+INT((Y-1)/4)
  ELSE
    F=F+INT(Y/4)-INT((.4*M)+2.3)
```

```
ENDIF
RETURN F
```

d) *FTOD*

```
FTOD:
LOCAL JF%,C,K,E%,ND
Y=INT(F/365.25)
ND=MOD:(F,365.25)
IF MOD:(Y,4.0)=0
  JF%=59
  ELSE
  JF%=58
ENDIF
IF ND<(JF%+1)
  M=(ND/31)+1
   D=MOD:(ND,31.0)+1
  RETURN
  ELSE
  ND=ND-JF%
  C=1
   DO
    K=1
    DO
      E%=MOD:(K,2.0)
      ND=ND-30-E%
      IF ND<=0
        D=ND+30+E%
        M=2+K+5*(C-1)
        RETURN
        ELSE
        K=K+1
      ENDIF
    UNTIL K=6
    C=C+1
  UNTIL C=3
ENDIF
```

5.7 Biorythms

BIO:, VBIO:()

What it does

Two of the routines used in the previous Chapter – GTDATE:() and DTOF: – can be used to evaluate the biorhythms for an individual, and that's what this two-procedure program does. Biorhythms are said to indicate an individual's Physical, Emotional and Intellectual state, and they're based on the fact(?) that these cycles run consistently from the date of birth. Each cycle lasts a different number of days: the Physical cycle is said to be 23 days long, the Emotional cycle 28 days long, and the Intellectual cycle 33 days long.

For the first half of each cycle, the status is 'positive' or in an active state, and for the second half the status is 'negative' or in a recuperative state. In each half, the 'peak' or 'trough' is reached mid-way.

The 'bad' days are said to be those where a cycle crosses from positive to negative and vice versa – and the 'danger days' are those where two cycles cross from positive to negative at the same time. What happens when all three cross together? Stay in bed! (This is a very rare event).

This program prints the percentage of maximum 'peak' or 'trough' in each cycle for the selected day – a minus sign indicates the troughs or recuperative periods. A zero percentage indicates a cross-over day.

A menu allows you to examine other days for the same birthdate, to enter a new birthdate, or simply to stop the program.

Note that, since the GTDATE:() function developed in the previous Chapter is used, the Birthdate is indicated by 'DATE 1' and the date for which you wish to examine the biorhythms is indicated as 'DATE 2'

There can be little doubt that 'biorhythms' actually exist: the human body's functions operate on numerous cycles. You can prove this for yourself with a simple test. Of the two nasal passages, one is normally in an active state, and the other in a recuperative state. By pressing a finger against the nose to close first one and then the other nasal passage whilst breathing in (through the nose), you should find that one of the nasal passages is 'more blocked' than the other. The cycle lasts around three hours – and so repeating the test three hours later should reveal the situation has reversed.

The question mark must come over the accuracy of the cycle period – and whether it is exactly the same for everyone. There is also the factor that long journeys involving jet-lag upset the body's cycles (isn't that what jet-lag is all about?) and consequently upset the predictability. Nevertheless, many people are strong advocates of Biorhythms, and will cite numerous instances where accidents and so on have occured during the 'danger days'.

With this program, you will be able to judge the predictability for yourself: if it 'works' for you, then your Organiser will be a remarkable instrument capable of giving you advance warning of when to take care, when to be creative, and so on.

Space required

The space required for the program, as listed, but without leading spaces or 'REMarks' (see Chapter 2.1) and excluding space required by any of the non-OPL routines called is:

a) *BIO*
Source + object code: 678 bytes
Object code only: 339 bytes

b) *VBIO:()*
Source + object code: 108 bytes
Object code only: 57 bytes

Both routines must be entered for the program to run

How it works

The Birth date is obtained by a call to GTDATE:(), and this is translated into the 'days-factor'. The second date is then obtained and converted, and the Birth date factor deducted from it to obtain the number of days the individual will have been alive on the required date. The days into each cycle are then obtained, by using the MOD:() utility to obtain the remainder after dividing the 'days-alive' value by the cycle length.

The next step is to obtain the percentage for each cycle, and display it. A fraction of '1' is obtained by a call in each instance to the second procedure, VBIO:(). This takes the number days into the cycle as a fraction of the cycle, finds out how many degrees that represents (360° representing one cycle), converts the degrees to radians so that the SIN can be taken (to get the fraction of '1'). This is fixed to two decimal places (who needs more?), and the value of the result is returned. It looks complicated, but it isn't really.

The decimal value returned is multiplied by a 100, to turn it into a percentage, and displayed along with a percentage sign. This is done for the three cycles, the first two being displayed on the top line by using the semi-colon technique. Then comes the menu selection: depending on the choice, a jump is made back to get a new date to examine, a new birthdate or to finish altogether.

Inputs

VBIO:() requires the number of days and the cycle length to be input as parameters.

Returns

VBIO:() returns a positive or negative decimal number representing the status as proportion of '+1' or '-1'

Non-OPL functions called

All these must also be entered for the 'BIO:' program to run.

GDATE:() (Chapter 5.6)
DTOF: (Chapter 5.6)
MOD:() (Chapter 2.13)

Globals

BIO: makes variables Y, M and D Global for use by GTDATE:() and DTOF:

Variables used

a) *Global*

Y = Year Holds the Year for the date calculation. .
M = Month Holds the Month for the date calculation.
D = Day Holds the day for the date calculation.

b) *Local*

P = Physical Holds the number of days into the Physical cycle
E = Emotional Holds the number of days into the Emotional cycle
I = Intellectual Holds the number of days into the Intellectual cycle.
FB = Factor Birthdate Holds the factor for the birthdate.
FD = Factor Date Holds the factor for the selected date.
C% = Choice Holds the selection from the menu.

Customizing

The program given here is really just the bare bones of what can be done. For example, you could add messages and so on concerning the states for each cycle, and you could even arrange for the program to provide a print-out of the cycle information for a given month.

The Listings

Enter the two procedures separately.

a) *BIO*

```
BIO:
GLOBAL Y,M,D
LOCAL P,E,I,FB,FD,C%
ST::
GTDATE:(1)      :REM Get Birth date
FB=DTOF:        :REM Convert to 'factor'
TD::
GTDATE:(2)      :REM Get 'test' date
FD=DTOF:        :REM Convert to 'factor'
FD=FD-FB        :REM Days 'alive'
P=INTF(MOD:(FD,23.0))  :REM Calculate each cycle
E=INTF(MOD:(FD,28.0))
I=INTF(MOD:(FD,33.0))
CLS
PRINT"P=";VBIO:(P,23.0)*100;
PRINT"% E=";VBIO:(E,28.0)*100
PRINT"I=";VBIO:(I,33.0)*100;"%"
GET
C%=MENU("SAMEB,NEWB,END")
IF C%=1
  GOTO TD::        :REM Get new 'test' date
ELSEIF C%=2
  GOTO ST::        :REM Get new Birth date
ENDIF
```

b) *VBIO*

```
VBIO:(D,C)
RETURN VAL(FIX$(SIN(RAD(360*D/C)),2,5))
```

5.8 When's Easter?

EASTER:

What it does

Here is a program that will tell you the date of Easter Sunday. To run it, simply enter the year on request. If you enter just two digits, '1900' will be added – so you can enter '88', for example, instead of 1988.

Space required

The space required for the procedure, as listed, but without leading spaces or 'REMarks' (see Chapter 2.1) and excluding space required by any of the non-OPL routines called is:
Source + object code: 947 bytes
Object code only: 452 bytes

How it works

This program was translated to the Organiser from a program developed several years ago for another computer. That program was developed from a method of calculating the date of Easter found in a magazine ... long since lost. So, the program is offered as it stands, without the underlying formulae or an explanation of the principles involved.

One line in the program may require an explanation (only one line?!):

```
IF (E%=24)+((E%=25)*(G%>11))
```

In this line the '+' and the '*' are the same as writing 'OR' and 'AND' respectively. The parts within each bracket are 'tests' which equate to '-1' if true, or zero if untrue. By substituting either of these values in place of the tests in the brackets, you will see that the result is the same when using the mathematical symbols as it is using the logical operators OR and AND.

The Listing

```
EASTER:
LOCAL A%,B%,C%,D%,E%,F%,G%,H%,J%,Y%
DO
  PRINT "WHICH YEAR"
  INPUT Y%
  IF Y%<100
    Y%=Y%+1900
  ENDIF
  G%=Y%-((Y%/19)*19)+1
  C%=1+(Y%/100)
  F%=(3*C%/4)-12
  A%=((8*C%+5)/25)-5
  D%=(5*Y%/4)-F%-10
  E%=11*G%+20+A%-F%
IF E%<0
    E%=E%+30
  ENDIF
  WHILE E%>29
    E%=E%-30
  ENDWH
  IF (E%=24)+((E%=25)*(G%>11))
    E%=E%+1
  ENDIF
  H%=44-E%
IF H%<21
    H%=H%+30
  ENDIF
  J%=D%+H%
  B%=J%-((J%/7)*7)
  H%=H%+7-b%
  CLS
  PRINT "EASTER ";Y%
  IF H%>31
    PRINT"SUNDAY APRIL ";H%-31
  ELSE
    PRINT"SUNDAY MARCH ";H%
  ENDIF
  GET
UNTIL MENU("MORE,END")<>1
```

APPENDICES

A1: OPL Commands & Functions

For convenience, all of the OPL commands and functions are listed here, together with brief descriptions, under headings related to their usage. For the full syntax and examples of use of each OPL word, please refer to your Manual.

File Handling

APPEND .... Add current record to the current file
BACK .... Make previous record in the file current
CLOSE .... Close current file
COPY .... Copy a file
COUNT .... Returns the number of records in current file
CREATE .... Creates a new file
DELETE F$ .... Delete file F$
DIR$ .... Display filenames
DISP() .... Display a record
EDIT S$ .... Edit string S$
EOF .... Marks file end
ERASE .... Delete the current record
EXIST(F$) ..... Test if file F$ exists
FIND(S$) .... Find string S$ in the current file
FIRST .... Make the first record in the file current
LAST .... Make the last record in the file current
NEXT .... Make the next record in the file current
OPEN .... Open an existing file
POS .... Returns 'number' of current record in the file
POSITION x .... Make record x in the file current
RECSIZE ...... Returns number of characters in current record
RENAME A$,B$ Rename file A$ as B$
UPDATE ...... Update the current record
USE .... Select a logic file for use

General

BEEP t%,n% .... Sound n% for t% x 20msecs
DATIM$ .... Returns current date and time as a string
DAY .... Returns day number in current month
FREE .... Returns memory left in RAM
HOUR .... Returns integer of current hour
MINUTE .... Returns integer of current minute
MONTH .... Returns integer of current month
SECOND .... Returns integer of current second
SPACE .... Returns memory left on current pack
YEAR .... Returns integer of current year

Input/Output

AT x%,y% .... Positions cursor at col x, line y
CLS .... Clears display
CURSOR on/off . Switches cursor display on/off
GET .... Waits for keypress, returns its ASCII value
GET$ .... Waits for keypress, returns the character
INPUT .... Input from keyboard until **EXE** pressed
KEY .... Returns ASCII value of a buffered keypress
KEY$ .... Returns character of a buffered keypress
KSTAT .... Set keyboard status
LPRINT .... Prints variable/string to connected printer
MENU(S$) ...... Displays S$ as Menu for selection
PRINT .... Prints variable/string on screen
VIEW(L%,S$) ... Displays S$ on line L%

Machine Code

ADDR(v) .... Returns address of variable v
ESCAPE off/on .. Prevents/allows program pausing
PEEKB(a%) ..... Returns the byte at address a%
PEEKW(a%) .... Returns the 'word' (two-bytes) at address a%
POKEB a%,c% .. Pokes byte c% at address a%
POKEW a%,c% . Pokes 'word' c% at address a%
USR(a%,b%) .... Passes b% to a user m/c routine at a%

Mathematical Functions

ABS(x) .... Returns absolute value of x
ATAN(x) .... Returns arctan of x
COS(x) .... Returns cosine of x
FLT(i%) .... Converts integer i% to floating point type
DEG(x) .... Converts x radians to degrees
EXP(x) .... Raises 'e' to the power x
HEX$(x%) ..... Returns hexadecimal value of decimal x%
IABS(x%) ...... Returns absolute value of integer x%
INT(x) .... Returns the integer of x
INTF(x) .... Returns the integer of x as a float type
LN(x) .... Returns log x to base 'e'
LOG(x) .... Returns log x to base 10
PI .... Returns pi = 3.14159265359
RAD(x) .... Converts x degrees to radians
RANDOMIZE x Sets fixed random sequence on x
RND .... Returns random decimal value between 0 and 1
SIN(x) .... Returns sin of x
SQR(x) .... Returns square root of x
TAN(x) .... Returns tangent of x

Program Control

AND .... Logical comparison
BREAK .... Breaks processing from a loop
CONTINUE .... Returns processing to top of loop
DO/UNTIL ..... Repeats processing till 'until' condition true
ERR .... Returns number of the last occuring error
ERR$(x%) ..... Returns a string describing error number x%
GLOBAL ...... Declares variables for the procedure
.... and subsequent procedures
GOTO j:: .... Jumps to label j::
IF/ELSEIF/ELSE Tests expression and acts accordingly
LABEL .... Specifies a point in a procedure
LOCAL .... Declares variables for the procedure
OFF .... Switch-off under program control
ONERR .... Error trapping
OR .... Logic comparison
PAUSE t% ..... Wait at keyboard for t% x 20ms
RAISE .... Simulates an error
REM .... Non-processing remark

RETURN v ...... .Return v (or v%, v$) from function
STOP .... .Break out of program
TRAP .... .Trap an error
WHILE/ENDWH .Repeats processing 'while' condition is true

String Handling

ASC(s$) .... .Returns ASCII of first character in s$
CHR$(n%) ...... .Returns character of n%
FIX$(v,d%,l%) . .Sets value v to d% decimal places in string l% long
GEN$(v,l%) ..... .Sets value v to a string l% long
LEFT$(s$,l%) ... .Returns left l% characters in s$
LEN(s$) .... .Returns length of string s$
LOC(S$,s$) ...... .Finds sub-string s$ in string S$
LOWER$(s$) .... .Converts string s$ to lower case characters
MID$(S$,s%,l%) .Returns l% characters from s% in S$
NUM$(v,l%) .... .Returns v as integer string l% long
REPT$(c$,r%) ... .Repeats string c$, r% times
RIGHT$(s$,l%) . .Returns l% characters from right of s$
SCI$(v,d%,l%) ... .Returns value v as a scientific string
UPPER$(s$) ..... .Converts string s$ to upper case characters
VAL(s$) .... .Returns value of s$

A2: Index of Routines

Utilities

Stock Control/Price List program

Banker – Bank Account program

General programs